CONFESSIONS
OF A
SEWER RAT

For my father, Francis Carty

CONFESSIONS OF A SEWER RAT

A Personal History of Censorship & The Irish Cinema

CIARAN CARTY

NEW
ISLAND
BOOKS
Dublin

Confessions of a Sewer Rat:
A Personal History of Censorship & the Irish Cinema
is first published in 1995 by
New Island Books
2, Brookside,
Dundrum Road,
Dublin 14,
Ireland

ISBN 1 874597 27 8

Photographs of John Boorman and Thaddeus O'Sullivan courtesy of *Sunday Tribune* photographers; photo of Jim Sheridan by Bryan Meade; photo of Joe Comerford by John Carlos; photo of Pat O'Connor by Ann Egan. Still from *Into the West* courtesy of Littlebird Ltd.; still from *Ann Devlin* courtesy of Pat Murphy and Aeon Films; stills from *Reefer And The Model* and *Angel* courtesy of Channel 4; still from *My Left Foot* courtesy of Ferndale Films Ltd.; still from *Ailsa* courtesy of Temple Films. Ciaran Carty and New Island Books express their appreciation to all copyright holders.

New Island Books receives financial assistance from
The Arts Council (An Chomhairle Ealaíon)
Dublin, Ireland.

Cover illustration by Jon Berkeley
Typeset by Graphic Resources
Printed in Ireland by Colour Books Ltd.

Contents

Much of the material on which this book is based has been published in various forms in *The Sunday Independent* and *The Sunday Tribune*. Virtually all quotations are from interviews and conversations with the author. They are intended to provide a personal and contemporaneous record of an Ireland that was changing from a country that suppressed movies in the 1960s and early 1970s to one that in the 1990s is now sucessfully creating them. *Confessions of a Sewer Rat* would not have been possible without the tolerance and support of the editors who gave me free rein over the years: George Hussey, Frank Staniforth, Hector Legge, Michael Hand, Aengus Fanning, Vincent Browne and Peter Murtagh. The tolerance and support of Julia Alonso Beazcochea will be evident from the text.

CHAPTER ONE

WE BURN BOOKS, DON'T WE?

The trunk was the size of a coffin. It was made of black wood with metal ribbing. It had belonged to the vicar of Bishop Auckland. He'd used it to ship bibles and evangelical tracts to India when he went out there as a missionary.

I bought it from his widow. She served me Darjeeling tea from a silver teapot. Everything in the vicarage was for sale. She had to clear out. The house wasn't hers; it went with the job. We agreed a price of ten shillings for the trunk, which she had advertised in the *Northern Despatch*, the Darlington evening newspaper where I worked as a sub-editor.

The trunk was now in a shed on the docks at the North Wall on the Dublin Quays. It had been forced open by customs officials on arrival from Liverpool on the B&I steamer *Munster*. They were not satisfied with my signed declaration that it contained "Personal Effects, no commercial value". Like sniffer dogs, they were trained to detect dangerous books. And they found them.

A card from the Revenue Commissioners, dated 11 June 1963, informed me that under Section 5 of the Censorship of Publications Act 1946, twelve "prohibited" books had been seized: *Butterfield 8* by John O'Hara, *The Big Sleep* by Raymond Chandler, *Cards of Identity* by Nigel Dennis, *The Catcher in the Rye* by JD Salinger, *Five* by Doris Lessing, *The Golden Ass* by Apuleius, *The Hucksters* by Frederic Wakeham, *The Law* by

Roger Vailland, *Memoirs of Hecate County* by Edmund Wilson, *The Philanderers* by Stanley Kaufmann, *The Strange Case of Miss Annie Spragg* by Louis Bromfield, and *Saturday Night and Sunday Morning* by Alan Sillitoe.

Before collecting the trunk, I checked with the Censorship Board at Merrion Square. It turned out that *Saturday Night and Sunday Morning* was not in fact banned.

A blue-suited customs official, in his thirties with Brylcreamed hair arranged in strands over the crown of his balding head, wasn't impressed. "Ah," he said, "but I am empowered by the Act not only to seize banned publications, but to seize any publication that I think is filthy and ought to be banned. That's why you can't have it."

I'd checked that also with the Censorship Board. Apparently this power only applied to "merchandise", not to a book that was part of the "personal baggage" of an incoming passenger.

The official glared at me.

"Well?" I said.

"Well what?"

"I'm entitled to have it returned to me."

Sensing his uncertainty, I added: "And you might also get me Doris Lessing's *Five*. It's not on the banned list either." I was bluffing, but it was worth a shot: anything to save *Five*, one of my favourite collections of stories.

He hesitated, then went to an office. I could hear muttering on a phone, then the receiver being banged down.

He came back with two paperbacks, *Saturday Night And Sunday Morning*, and *Five*. I reached across the counter and pulled them from his hand. "You have to sign for them." I put my name on the receipt with a flourish.

"What will happen to the other books you have seized?"

"They'll be taken to Dublin Castle and eventually burned," he smirked, his confidence restored.

A B&I official helped me carry the trunk from the warehouse and wedge it into the boot of my father's Mini. It stuck out of the back of the car like a fat cigar, gripped between the lips of the half-shut door.

"I've never seen that happen before, somebody getting their books back like that," he said.

"Does this happen a lot? Do they seize much?"

"Yeah, they're at it all the time."

He flicked through *Saturday Night And Sunday Morning*. "I've heard about this one, it's a fillum, isn't it?"

"Yes. It's an even better read, though. Do you read much?"

"Yeah, all the time."

"Well, keep it. That's what it's for."

Julia looked relieved when I got back to our flat on Pembroke Road. "I thought I wouldn't see you again, I thought you would be arrested," she said. That's what all too likely could have happened in the Spain she'd left to marry me. Under Franco, you didn't challenge authority. Her father had been involved with the Republicans during the Civil War, her cousin had grown up in a refugee camp in France, an uncle had been kept hidden for two years in a cellar to avoid arrest and execution. I'd joked about bringing her to a free country. Now I wasn't so sure.

A month after we returned from our honeymoon in France, two Special Branch men had arrived at the door to deport her. She had kept her Spanish citizenship. We hadn't noticed that her passport, still in her maiden name, had been stamped at Dublin airport, only granting her permission to remain in Ireland for thirty days. We showed the Special Branch men our wedding certificate. They were sympathetic but we still had to go to the Aliens Office at Dublin Castle for questioning before the legality of her status was officially recognised.

Julia helped me drag the trunk up the four flights of stairs to the flat, which overlooked the kiosk at the corner of Pembroke Road. On the opposite side exotic trees from the old Trinity

College botanic gardens were being chopped down to make way for the new American Intercontinental Hotel, later known as Jury's.

The Dublin I'd come home to was at the beginning of a property development boom that would see much of its Georgian architecture and character destroyed.

We unlatched the trunk. It was crammed with paperbacks and newspapers I hadn't wanted to part with when I was leaving Darlington. I made a gesture of replacing Doris Lessing's *Five*, a banned book, in the vicar's trunk. "What are you laughing at?" Julia asked. Then she laughed too. "Nobody is going to burn my books," I said.

* * * * * *

An absurd irony was that all the seized books had come originally from Dublin. You could pick up almost anything if you browsed long enough in Greene's second-hand bookshop or in Webbs on the quays. They provided respite from the tedium of listening to George O'Brien and James Meehan lecture on the Banking Commission Report or arcane Keynesian economic theory at UCD.

The fact that a book might be banned was never much of an inconvenience. Even as a child I'd been able to read whatever books I wanted. The house on Sandymount Avenue, just down from where WB Yeats once lived, was spilling over with them. My father, Frank Carty, wrote novels and radio plays. Graham Greene had praised his *Legion of the Rearguard* as an eyewitness account of the Civil War that "is always interesting, often exciting and presents what history cannot do, the curious mental contrasts of a local, a provincial war, the shy romantic prudish affections of gunmen on the run."

During World War II he joined with Sean O'Faolain in abridging a hundred classic novels — all the greats by Bronte, Thackeray, Dickens, Collins, Scott, Hugo, Dumas, Hawthorne,

Cooper — for a special cheap paperback edition for sale to British troops, a market shrewdly identified by fellow Wexford man JJ O'Leary, founder of the Parkside Press. A full set of the books accumulated in the garage, an Aladdin's cave of other worlds that I was to discover and explore through much of childhood.

O'Leary also launched the *English* and *Irish Digests*, local ripoffs of the successful Reader's Digest format. My father, who edited them, would give me a shilling if I spotted any item worth publishing.

Tipped off by the Holy Ghost fathers, who ran mission schools in West Africa, O'Leary came up with the idea of publishing textbooks in the various African languages: up to then everything taught in African schools was in English. Maurice Macmillan — his father Harold Macmillan was to signal the end of colonialism in Africa with his 'Winds of Change' speech in 1959 — saw its potential for the Macmillan publishing company and provided distribution backup. Father went out to Nigeria to open up the market.

Later, during the Biafran War in the late 1960s, some of his African contacts came to me with photographs of atrocities — bombed hospitals and schools — which I published in the *Sunday Independent*, accusing the Irish Government of trying to cover up what was happening there.

In 1957, when a new IRA campaign of violence broke out along the Border, the Taoiseach, Eamon De Valera, called my father to Leinster House. They hadn't seen each other for years: he'd been one of Dev's commandants in Wexford during the War of Independence. "Frank," Dev said, "I'm worried about the *Irish Press*. They're becoming unreliable in their treatment of the IRA. Will you take over as editor?" "Yes", said my father, without hesitating, even though it meant dropping his publishing career. The meeting lasted a couple of minutes. Nothing more needed to be said. De Valera's strength was the loyalty he could command.

When the *Sunday Press* published picture spreads romanticising the IRA's activities, my father for a while found himself editing both newspapers: this was just before I returned from England in 1962 to work on the rival *Sunday Independent*.

A recurring memory of my father is waiting to see the books and magazines he'd bring home from work in his battered leather briefcase. The 'Talk of the Town' column in *The New Yorker* was an initiation to the world of chic put-downs. I'd draw Irish variations on the Butch cartoons from the *Saturday Evening Post*.

A crony of my father, Eoin O'Keeffe, who was my godfather, had a bookshop in Westmoreland Street. Every birthday I'd get the tram into town to select just one book as a present. The joy of it was that it would take all day to make up my mind, rummaging through all the shelves over and over again.

I lived as much in the imagination as in any outside reality. On walks with my father on Sandymount strand, we'd concoct plots for plays we might some day write together. He'd go over my stories, which I typed on his old upright Remington typewriter, unobtrusively suggesting improvements. "Avoid the word very," he'd say. "Never use 'I' if you can help it." While I was still at school at Blackrock College my first story 'The Devil's Guarantee' — Damon Runyan in style but with an O'Henry twist ending — was published in the *Evening Herald*, earning me £3. My caricatures of Irish people who had become famous abroad as celebrities were accepted as illustrations for a 'This Other Ireland' column he contributed to the *Irish Press* in the early 1950s.

He was the only person with whom I could talk about what I really felt. He was a small, fragile man. I never heard him shout. As a boy of sixteen he caught the train to Dublin, hoping to join the Easter Rising. He got off too soon — he'd never been out of Wexford before — and the Rising was over before he could find it.

When he got back home a motion before Wexford Corporation called on the authorities to deal with the rebel leaders with the utmost severity. His father, who was an alderman, proposed an amendment that lenience be shown to their followers. The Redmondites promptly boycotted the family store on Main Street in protest at this betrayal of their class.

Father fired the first shots in the Black and Tan war in Wexford Town. He acquired an old Lugar with some bullets and would prowl outside the British Army barracks in the darkness of night, letting off the gun at intervals. Later he'd intercept the mail at Rosslare. Letters home from young Tommies would talk about being surrounded by wild Fenians and unable to leave the barracks.

After the Ceasefire, they buried their arms, suspicious of Collins and the Treaty. On De Valera's instructions he and his men dug them up again after the Four Courts was attacked. Father was captured in an ambush by a man who had fought beside him against the Tans. He was interned at Portlaoise, spending weeks on hunger strike after burning his cell.

He became the prison barber, a talent he had acquired from his father who in 1896 had opened the first modern hair salon on Wexford's Main Street: it proudly offered clients all the latest styling techniques and creams. Until I left home, my father always cut my hair.

He was a heavy smoker — up to eighty a day: he couldn't write without a cigarette between his lips, much to the disapproval of Tom Reilly, his doctor and a friend from childhood. On walks he'd pause and catch his breath and I'd have the awful foreboding that he was going to die. There were nights when I'd wake up in a sweat at the thought of losing him.

One night when I was seven or eight and lying in bed listening to the murmur of voices downstairs, I heard him cry out in pain. I cowered in terror beneath the sheets. An ambulance came. He was taken to hospital for an emergency appendix operation. Later he tried to reassure me by describing what had happened.

I fainted. For years afterwards I'd pass out at the mere mention of blood.

There were times in the cinema when I'd suddenly go cold and have to put my head down between my legs to keep conscious. I once passed out in O'Connell Street after a film preview. When I opened my eyes people were walking by, as if I wasn't there. One man even stepped over me.

When the point of a knife was drawn across a pregnant Mia Farrow's stomach in *Rosemary's Baby* during a club screening at the Guinness Film Society — it had been banned by the Censor — I had to sneak out to the lavatory.

My father got me work as a stringer for Don Higgins of United Press International when I left college. I'd no intention of becoming an economist. I'd only taken a degree in politics and economics because he said it would a good idea to do something I might not otherwise bother about, if only to be able to tell when experts were talking rubbish. He'd always regretted that he hadn't. He was right. I came away realising that economics was little more than intelligent guesswork. All its statements are necessarily relative and dependent on an unpredictable human factor.

Higgins would ring up at a moment's notice with sports assignments. I'd get on my bicycle and pedal across town to Santry Stadium to cover Herb Elliott's attempt to break the world record for the mile — he didn't — and then back again to the Radio Eireann newsroom at the GPO to wire off a report to Australian newspapers.

An attempt to start a show page on the *Munster Tribune* in Clonmel — circulation 10,000 — where I got a summer job as a reporter in 1959, was equally inglorious. The local cinema manager threatened to withdraw advertising if I dared to criticise any of his movies. Reproducing film stills was deemed an extravagance by editor George Hussey. I had to order free blocks provided film distributors in Dublin. By the time they arrived, the paper would have gone to press.

Nobody on the *Northern Despatch* in Darlington, which I joined in the biting cold of 1960, could pronounce Ciaran: I became known as Norbert, a confirmation name, soon abbreviated to Nobby, which made me sound like a footballer. It was like taking on another identity. My bank account at the Midland was in the new name. Julia, who had come to Darlington as an *au pair* thinking it was a suburb of London — only to get off the train six hours later in the biting North Sea cold of Bank Top station — called me Norberto, as did her family when I pursued her back to Madrid.

By then I had become film critic, a job no one wanted because it involved night work at no extra pay. It led to a TV debut — I'd never even seen a TV set — judging the North East heat for Miss Britain.

We were required to walk up and down a line of girls in bathing costumes, taking notes: it was like a scene from one of those slave auctions in the Deep South. Another night I had to present a darts trophy at a Working Mens Club, after which the President wanted to slip me a half-crown as a tip.

The editor Frank Staniforth allowed considerable latitude in what I wrote. While critics in London were being snooty about the excessive violence and sexual explicitness of Hitchcock's *Psycho*, I made it the *Despatch*'s movie of the year. "Are you sure about that?" Staniforth asked, worried about the furore. "After all, you're only twenty-one and it's been widely criticised." "Yes," I said. He didn't just print the piece, he went to see the movie.

Several people walked out in the middle of a performance of *The Hostage* at the Hippodrome in Stockton. So the *Despatch* leapt to Brendan Behan's defence. "If it is blasphemy to exhort Khruschev not to Muck About With The Bomb, then *The Hostage* stands condemned," I wrote. "If it is obscene to criticise the shooting of innocent people in the name of patriotism, then Brendan Behan deserves the castigation he has received."

Sean Lemass had succeeded Dev as Taoiseach in 1959 just before I left on the boat for England. The Economic Programme for Expansion he had introduced as Minister for Finance with Ken Whitaker soon showed signs of transforming Ireland into an urban, industrial society. Tax exemptions attracting substantial foreign investment boosted output, and emigration began to fall off. The gloom of the 1950s began to give way to a boom culture. It seemed a challenging time to return to Ireland.

Hector Legge, editor of the *Sunday Independent* since 1940 and one of the great figures in Irish journalism — he'd rushed John A Costello into declaring Ireland a Republic in 1949 with a pre-emptive "scoop" — provided the chance in autumn 1961 with a typically flamboyant ad for a "dynamic young" journalist in *World Press News*.

When I applied, he telegrammed: INTERVIEW FRIDAY 4.30 LEGGE. Not to be outdone, I telegrammed back: YES. CARTY. He shook hands after the interview: "The job is yours." Later, he rang me: "The board have told me to cancel your appointment. They've discovered that your father is the editor of the *Sunday Press*. They say you would have a conflict of loyalty if you worked for us." Then he paused dramatically, one of his favourite mannerisms. "I told them I had given you my word. The appointment stands."

* * * * * *

Doris Lessing's *Five* and Alan Sillitoe's *Saturday Night and Sunday Morning* had been freed on a technicality. The other ten books still stood condemned, awaiting burning. Even murderers on Death Row could hope for a last minute reprieve. I owed them that chance.

Charles Haughey as Minister for Justice had the ultimate authority to grant one. Since his appointment in 1961 at the age of thirty-six, he had being making his name as a dynamic minister, pushing forward law reform. He'd clamped down ruthlessly on the IRA by reactivating the special Criminal Courts: within a year they were forced to call off their Border campaign. He epitomised the progressive pragmatic approach of the Lemass era, his flamboyant lifestyle and rapidly acquired fortune as an accountant daringly at odds with the puritanical ethos that had characterised the De Valera years. I'd never met him but once had seen him in the Gresham Hotel having tea with some nuns. He looked up and winked at my father. "Be wary of people who wink," Father told me.

I wrote to Haughey expressing dismay at the seizure of the books, pointing out that most of them had been bought originally in Ireland and that they were for my own personal use as a writer and journalist. I suggested that the Censorship Act was out of date and ought not apply to literature.

My letter was promptly acknowledged, and on 24 July I received a letter from John Olden, an official in the Department of Justice: "I am directed to inform you by the Minister for Justice in reference to your letter of 15 July and to enclose a permit for the importation of the following prohibited publications — *Cards of Identity*, *The Golden Ass*, *The Catcher In The Rye*, *The Law*, *The Big Sleep*, *Memoirs of Hecate County*, *Butterfield 8*, *The Philanderers*, *The Hucksters*, *The Strange Case of Miss Annie Spragg*.

Armed with the permit, I went immediately to Dublin Castle and presented it to an official at the Office of the Revenue Commissioners. He looked at the letter doubtfully.

"This is most irregular."

"It has been issued by the Minister for Justice."

He went away and after a long delay came back with my books. "If it had been a few days later, they would have been burned," he told me.

I brought the ten books home and symbolically put them back in the trunk with Doris Lessing's *Five*. It had been a victory of sorts. It should have satisfied me. But it didn't. I had got my books back, but they were still banned. And how many other books and writers were banned?

About the only good thing that could be said about the Censorship of Publications Act was that all decisions made by the Censorship Board had to be published. In practice the Board did the minimum required to meet this stipulation. Lists of banned books were issued without comment to the newspapers and generally appeared as small paragraphs buried on a back page. But any member of the public was free to go to the Board's office in Merrion Square and inspect its lists. So I did.

I was shown to a room and several ledgers were brought to me. Inscribed in each of them in elegant ink script were the author, title and date of every publication banned since the Act was introduced in 1929.

It took me a few days but I went through every page, making notes. Over 10,000 books were listed. It was like a roll call of twentieth-century literature. William Faulkner, Jean Paul Sartre, Thomas Mann, Ernest Hemingway, John Steinbeck, Sinclair Lewis, John Dos Passos, Thomas Wolfe, James Farrell, Frank O'Connor, Sean O'Faolain...

Among the more recent entries were Joseph Heller's *Catch 22*, William Styron's *Set House On Fire*, Philip Roth's *Letting Go*, JP Donleavy's *A Singular Man*, Irish Murdoch's *A Severed Head*, James Baldwin's *Giovanni's Room*, Shirley Ann Grau's *The Hard Blue Sky*, Herbert Gold's *Salt*, and Edna O'Brien's *The Country Girls*.

When the banned short story writer Frank O'Connor had been sacked from his job in a Dublin public library because of what were termed as irregularities in his private life — he had left his wife for another woman — Hector Legge had stood by him, giving him a column in the *Sunday Independent* (an act of some courage, given the fact that TV Murphy, proprietor of the paper, was a prominent lay Catholic).

Legge beamed with mischief when I filled him in on what had being happening. "Write it," he said. The article that appeared, one of the first to detail the full range of the Censorship Board's decisions, was illustrated by a photograph of the ten books seized at Customs and reprieved by Charles Haughey. "The fact that outstanding works of literature are put on a par with pornographic filth is a slur on their authors and a slur on Ireland," I wrote.

Legge was also prepared to take a stand in 1965 when the young writer John McGahern's first novel *The Dark* was banned and McGahern, who had separated from his wife, was sacked from his job as a teacher at a North-side national school.

At a seminar on censorship at the Irish Film Centre in 1995, McGahern recalled being interviewed at the time by the secretary of the Irish National Teachers Organisation, a Mr Kellagher, who told him: "If it was just the ould book, then maybe we might have been able to do something for ya, but going and marrying this foreign woman in a registry office, you have turned yourself into an impossible case entirely." McGahern still feels the hurt. "I came to whatever intellectual age I am in the Dublin of the late 1950s and early 1960s. Church and State had colluded to bring about a climate that was insular, repressive and sectarian. The country was being run almost exclusively for a small Catholic middle class, and its church.

"I belong to the first generation to be born into this free State, and it grew clear that the whole, holy situation was of our own making. Britain could no longer be blamed. In fact, certain British institutions like Penguin Books, the BBC, the *Observer*, became our windows to the world.

"We discovered that most of the books being banned were not worth reading. Those that were could be easily found and were quickly passed around. My belief is that literary censorship is nearly always foolish, since it succeeds in attracting attention to what it seeks to suppress. There is no taste so tantalising as that of forbidden fruit."

By that time I had become a stringer for the Copley feature agency in the US. I filed a report on the McGahern banning and on the philistine nature of the Censorship Act. It appeared in about fifty different English and Spanish language newspapers across America, together with the photograph of my seized books. The tactic was that perhaps by embarrassing the Government abroad, they might eventually feel shamed into bringing the Censorship Board to heel.

In 1967 an amending Act passed into law which provided that if a book was banned for being indecent or obscene, the ban would automatically expire twelve years after its imposition. A book could however be re-banned. Bans would still stand on any publication advocating "the unnatural prevention of conception or the procurement of abortion or miscarriage or the use of any method, treatment or appliance for the purpose of such prevention or procurement."

The amendment had the immediate effect of freeing the vast majority of titles on the banned list. Nobody any longer needed Charles Haughey's permission to read *The Catcher In The Rye* or Apuleius's *The Golden Ass*. Even better, it soon became clear that the Censorship Board had been instructed to adopt a more liberal approach. The days of banning literature were all but over.

CHAPTER TWO

HOLLYWOOD ON THE LIFFEY:

PART ONE

1

I Found It At The Movies

The man carefully sets the timer on the bomb. The clock begins to tick. Grabbing the girl's hand, he runs with her towards the exit to the bunker, a gleam of light in the distance. A siren goes off. German soldiers swarm into the tunnel in pursuit. Bullets ricochet off the walls. The metal door starts to close. Just before it clangs shut, he desperately pushes the girl through, then squeezes through himself. They roll down a steep slope, falling into each other's arms. There is an expectant silence. A blinding flash fills the screen.

Maybe it was a Ronald Colman or a Leslie Howard movie. I've never been able to track it down. When you're six or seven you just remember images, not names. And the images stay with you forever. Like the sight of Japanese soldiers over-running the last American trench in *Wake Island*, to which I was taken by a Benedictine cousin of my father just after the War: it made me think of Jimmy Hill's dad, whose tongue had been cut out when he was taken prisoner in Burma.

My mother didn't like me going to films. She thought the cinema was common. Her sister Aggie had disgraced the family by playing the piano for silent films at the Carlton cinema. Their father had been an official in Dublin Corporation. He wore stiff white collars and a black suit. He was ahead of his time in sending my mother to university and allowing her to go to Paris by herself when she was twenty. She studied piano with the legendary Miss Reid: this was a time when the parlour music tradition that nurtured James Joyce was still commonplace in

Dublin. She played from the heart rather than the head, not bothered if she missed some notes, just reaching for the feeling of a piece. I'd go to sleep at night listening her play Liszt and Chopin in the room below or accompanying my Aunt May, who had a beautiful soprano voice and won prizes at the *Feis Ceoil*. I can still remember every word of Ivor Novello's 'Dream of Olwyn' and 'Ma Bella Margaritha'.

The Shaw family moved in next door early in the War. Major Tom was away serving with the British Army: we weren't to see him until 1946, when he returned driving the first car anyone had seen for years.

Babs Shaw, left alone with four children, was bored. She'd pay us sixpence to find out the programme changes at the nearby Ritz cinema — better known as the Shack. We'd walk along the railway tracks from Sandymount Avenue and copy out details of the films from posters in the foyer. We'd give her a synopsis of the programme so she could decide what she wanted to see. Sometimes she didn't get out of bed until the afternoon. If she was in good mood, she'd embarrass us by giving us big lipsticky kisses.

We used the money to go to Saturday matinees. I'd pretend to my mother that I was going for a jog. All our gang, led by Paddy Shaw, wanted to be athletes. We staged the Olympic Games in the back garden. It wasn't just day-dreaming: one of the older boys, Ronnie Delaney, went on to win a gold medal in the 1,500 metres at the Melbourne Olympics several years later.

Cinema was like a forbidden fruit, although my mother told me years later she'd always known what we were up to. Aunt May shared my secret. She'd take me on the tram to town to the Capitol cinema, which had the added attraction of a restaurant where you could have egg and chips before the main programme.

Sandymount in the 1940s and early 1950s was still a village. When we got the tram to Dublin we'd say we were "going into town". Milk and bread were delivered each day by horse-drawn vans.

We'd moved to the house near the railway station on Sandymount Avenue in 1941. Having to cycle in and out of town every night from Mount Merrion to the *Irish Press*, where he was then a sub-editor, had become too exhausting for my father. Tom Reilly, who had a doctor's petrol allowance, helped us move some of our things in his black V8.

Cinema was an escape from the insularity of suburban Dublin, a chance to experience other exotic and more dangerous worlds where beautiful and flagrantly available women drove along highways in open convertibles with their blonde hair flowing in the wind. The nearest we got to an available woman as ten-year-olds was queuing to kiss a girl called Olive behind the pavilion at Pembroke cricket club.

We were the last generation before television. On Pathé newsreels we saw the first shocking images of the Nazi death camps, the frightening beauty of mushroom clouds from atomic explosions, the waves of American troops massing on the snow-swept 49th Parallel as the Korean War turned nasty.

Aunt May loved Hollywood pictures. The English ones, with their gentility and drabness, were too like the life she knew, living alone in a flat, working in the Civil Service. She was a frustrated romantic. Mother told me that she's been unlucky in love. She found it instead at the movies.

You didn't see continental movies at the Shack or the Capitol. I was seventeen before I was initiated to their delights by Florence Ryan, a pianist friend of my sister. She took me to Renoir's *La Grande Illusion* at the Astor. And then there was Bardem's *Death of A Cyclist* and that shot of a car speeding along a road lined with trees. And the clock with no hands in Bergman's *Wild Strawberries*. And the waif-like beauty of Giulietta Massina's face in Fellini's *White Sheik*. I was entranced. It opened up a whole new language of cinema. I began reading newspaper reviews, but most of them read like blurbs. I'd try to recapture and prolong in my own words the sensations I experienced watching movies.

2

The Irish Film Industry
That Wasn't

Elizabeth Taylor sipped a pint of Guinness in a bar near Ardmore Studios in Bray, County Dublin. "It's no stunt," she said, "I like it." She was killing time while husband Richard Burton finished a fight scene for the John Le Carre thriller *The Spy Who Came In From The Cold*.

Burton didn't delay to have his make-up removed afterwards, and arrived at the pub with a big bloody bruise under his eye. "I'd like to see anyone risk a fight with me," he said. No one did.

Students gaped as a chauffeur-driven Rolls Royce pulled up in front of the main Earlsfort Terrace entrance to University College Dublin. "I'm looking for the debating hall," said a tall, blond American getting out. It was George Peppard, guest speaker at a meeting of the Literary and Historical Debating Society. He'd been invited along by students acting with him as extras for £5 a day on the World War I movie *The Blue Max*, shooting on location in the Wicklow mountains and the costliest movie yet to be made in Ireland.

Sean Lemass had helped lure the $6 million Twentieth Century Fox production to Ireland early in 1966 by offering the services of 1,000 Irish soldiers for the battle scenes that provide the backdrop to spectacular dog-fight action sequences. Photographed during a visit to Ardmore to see rushes of some of the scenes, Lemass reiterated that he was anxious to attract more foreign productions to the studios. He regarded cinema as a potentially important export industry which had already brought in $3 million in foreign currency the previous year.

With the glitter of visiting stars came a greater tolerance towards movies, which was reflected in moves to liberalise the notoriously rigid censorship system. Charles Haughey's successor as Minister for Justice in 1965, the thirty-four-year-old lawyer Brian Lenihan, set up a completely new Film Appeals Board with power to release with limited certificates movies that previously had been rejected as subversive of public morality. Frank dialogue, references to homosexuality, abortion and birth control, controversial social themes and the depiction of nudity could now be passed for Over 18 audiences.

Even more significantly there was no public outcry from Catholic pressure groups when previously banned movies like *What's Up Pussycat*, *The Ceremony*, *The Party's Over*, *The Loudest Whisper*, *The Collector* and *Room At the Top* (eight years after its release in the UK) reached the screens.

By luck I had just become film critic for the *Sunday Independent*. Des Hickey, for whom I used to deputise, wanted more time to write screenplays. His brother Kieran Hickey, who trained at the London Film School, had returned to Ireland and set up his own production company.

The same week I was appointed, Julia gave birth to our first child, Francis, and a strike closed down all the national newspapers. I spent the summer going to movies to write reviews that were never to appear.

Despite its popularity with audiences — per capita Ireland, with 41.2 million cinema admissions and 283 cinemas, was one of the world's top movie-going nations — the only Irish movies up to then were recycled Irish theatrical triumphs. Ardmore Studios had been set up in 1958 primarily as a means of putting Abbey Theatre plays on the screen, and although the Studios were now servicing a flow of international productions, they did nothing to stimulate Irish film production.

While Ireland was widely appreciated as a location for films — Laurence Olivier used it for the battle scenes in *Henry V* (among the extras was future playwright Hugh Leonard), John Ford immortalised the Atlantic landscapes in *The Quiet Man* — the idea that Irish film-makers ought to produce movies of their own dealing with contemporary Irish themes was dismissed as unrealistic.

As recently as 1964 the studios had gone into receivership. Now, having serviced and built sets for *Ballad In Blue, Young Cassidy, The Face of Fu Manchu* and *Ten Little Indians*, as well as the big budget *The Spy Who Came In From The Cold* and *The Blue Max*, there was a new optimism. Dublin was beginning to be talked about abroad as Hollywood on the Liffey.

Telefis Eireann launched Ireland into the TV era in 1962. Social and sexual taboos were being aired in homes in the most remote corners of the country via Gay Byrne's 'Late Late Show'. Donogh O'Malley, the radical-minded Minister for Education, was about to introduce free secondary schools. It seemed in keeping with this spirit of moving forward that Ireland should develop its own film industry.

But Ardmore was only an illusion of a film industry. When the Elizabeth Taylors and George Peppards moved on to other movies, the studios were left waiting for telephone calls. There was no indigenous film-making to sustain them.

Lemass was concerned only with the economic potential of Ardmore Studios. His instinctive solution to any Irish industrial shortcoming was to build a factory. As early as 1943 he had proposed the setting up of a studio as a facility for the use of foreign producers, only to be rebuffed by Finance Minister Frank Aiken, who argued: "If this country is going to spend money on the film business, it should be spent on the production of Irish films by Irish organisations."

Lemass had got his way in 1958 when Emmet Dalton and Louis Ellman bought a thirty-five acre estate near Bray on which they built the three sound stages and recording theatre with dubbing and mixing facilities that were to comprise Ardmore Studios. They were funded by a grant of £45,000 from the Industrial Development Authority and a loan of £217,000 from the Industrial Credit company, both of which were approved by Lemass as Minister for Industry and Commerce.

Their plan was to produce filmed versions of Abbey Theatre plays for the American market. The Irish Film Finance Corporation was set up to offer funding inducements for international film producers to use Ardmore's facilities.

The rub was that in order to become eligible for Eady production finance, Ardmore was treated as a UK studio and was restricted to employing members of the English ACTT film technicians union. Irish technicians were effectively excluded from working at Ardmore. There was virtually no Irish technical or creative input into movies filmed at Ardmore. And most of the films made there in the 1960s were about somewhere else.

Even on the screen there was little or no hint of Ireland. The Julie Andrews romance *Darling Lili* appropriated Trinity's College's historic quadrangle and camouflaged it to pass for German World War I military headquarters. Kilkenny was transformed into eighteenth-century London, complete with sedan chairs, for *Lock Up Your Daughters*. A 300-foot wide replica outline of a white horse, the famous English landmark, was cut into the Galway hillside to provide a backdrop to David Hemmings's *Alfred The Great*.

John Huston, who had become an Irish citizen in 1964 and lived in a twenty-room mansion near Galway where he delighted in riding to the hounds, went out of his way to make films in Ireland. *The List Of Adrian Messinger* and *Casino Royale* were partially shot there because he refused to work anywhere else. He persuaded MGM to let him shoot the highwayman period romp *Sinful Davey* entirely on location in Donegal and the Wicklow mountains. "It will plough millions into the Irish economy," he said.

Unlike Irish politicians, he realised that bringing large film crews from the US or Britain at irregular intervals was not enough. He wanted the Irish to get involved themselves.

"After nearly seventy years of movie history, Ireland, almost alone among nations, has no movie industry." he complained.

His solution had an un-Irish directness. He invited Jack Lynch, who had succeeded Lemass as Taoiseach in 1966, to lunch on the set of *Sinful Davey* and told him: "It's high time Ireland had her own film industry." Then he produced a blueprint. "This is how it can be done," he told an astonished Lynch. He dismissed Ardmore studios as "a financial disaster."

Before Lynch left the set he had promised to give careful consideration to everything Huston had proposed. "I too believe Ireland has a future in movie-making," he said.

When Connemara-born Peter O'Toole heard of Huston's plan, he promptly flew to Ireland to talk to President Eamon de Valera. "I'll do anything I can to help," he said.

Meanwhile Lynch was as good as his word. A committee was set up with Huston as chairman to look into ways of setting up a film industry in Ireland. Its members included Lord Killanin, who had worked with John Ford on *The Quiet Man* and *The Rising Of the Moon*, and the documentary film-makers Patrick Carey, Tom Hayes and Louis Marcus. Marcus argued forcefully that an elaborate studio was "the last thing we need to become a feature-producing country."

Within a year the committee produced a report recommending the setting up of a film board to provide pre-production finance for international productions and for smaller budget Irish productions, and to encourage the production in Ireland of television commercials. A Film Industry Bill was published in 1970 to bring this into effect.

However the deteriorating situation in the streets of the North was dragging the Ireland back to the sectarian politics many thought had been consigned to history by the Republic's imminent entry into full membership of the Common Market.

Progressive legislative reforms that were designed to help the Republic evolve into a modern pluralist European society began to be sidelined as more and more of the Dail's time was taken up with Partition politics.

On 5 October 1968, about 2,000 supporters of the Civil Rights movement took part in a banned march through Derry in support of their demands for an end to sectarian discrimination against Catholics in housing, jobs and education. On reaching Craigavon bridge they were baton-charged by the Royal Ulster Constabulary. As the marchers turned back in panic and tried to disperse down Duke Street they ran into another baton charge. That night the barricades went up in the Catholic Bogside. The spiral of violence that was to result in over a quarter-century of suffering and killing in the North had begun.

Emotions ran high in the Republic in 1969 over sectarian attacks on Northern Catholic areas by loyalist mobs, apparently abetted by the RUC. There was inflammatory talk about sending troops across the border to protect them. The Taoiseach Jack Lynch assured the Dail that his government would "not stand idly by". Various covert operations by Irish Army Intelligence to defend Catholic areas were initiated.

Derry Civil Rights activist Eamonn McCann was approached by an Irish Army officer in September 1969 and asked to take part in military training in Donegal. Belfast IRA man John Kelly, who went with Captain James Kelly of Irish Military Intelligence to meet a ship *City of Dublin* in March 1970, believed he was part of a fully-fledged government operation with orders to move guns from it to Catholic areas in the north.

In 1970 Hector Legge unexpectedly called me into his office before the usual Saturday morning news conference. It was 2 May. *Sunday Independent* political correspondent Ned Murphy, a close friend of the Fine Gael leader of the opposition, Liam Cosgrave, was with him.

"What would you say if I told you that we have gardai information that quantities of arms are being illegally imported into the country for use in the North with the complicity of certain Government Ministers?" he said.

"Which ministers?"

"Haughey, Blaney, Boland and O Morain."

Ned sat to one side, a glum expressive on his face.

If true, it would have been one of the most sensational scoops ever published in an Irish newspaper. The political repercussions were awesome. The Government would probably fall. Haughey's ambitions to become Taoiseach would surely be ruined forever.

"Will it stand up?"

"Yes," said Legge.

Ned grunted. I got the impression a decision had already been taken.

Legge paused for several seconds, with his usual flair for the dramatic. Then he announced: "We're not publishing. We have other responsibilities. The country is on the knife edge of civil war. This belongs in the Dail. It's up to Cosgrave to confront Lynch."

Having failed to leak the story in the *Sunday Independent*, Cosgrave did just that. Lynch promptly dismissed Haughey as Minister for Finance and Blaney as Minister for Agriculture. He accepted the resignations of O'Morain as Minister for Justice and Boland as Minister for Local Government and Social Welfare. After a thirty-seven hour debate, the Dail applauded Lynch's call for moderation and the threat of a constitutional crisis was averted. The Government won a vote on the appointment of new ministers. Haughey and Blaney were arrested on arms conspiracy charges on 28 May and released later on bail. They were cleared of all charges and acquitted in the subsequent Arms Trial.

Amid the hysteria — apparently at once stage Lynch even feared a possible coup — and the inevitable confusion with so many new ministers trying to find their feet, the Film Bill failed to get a second reading and was quietly shelved.

It would be ten years before it was back on the table.

Yet it is doubtful if it would have provided the basis for a viable Irish film industry even if it had gone through, as it sought to set up the apparatus for an industry before there was anyone capable of taking proper advantage of it. Ireland had a handful of directors like Patrick Carey, Louis Marcus and Kieran Hickey, but their experience was almost entirely in documentaries. RTE was still in the process of training producers and directors, and possessed only a small pool of cameramen and trained technicians.

There was nothing in the output of the small group of independent film-makers to suggest the emergence of writers and directors capable of creating movies that could appeal to international audiences. The Government itself gave no real indication that it appreciated the creative potential of cinema. On the contrary, despite the apparent reforms of censorship in 1965, they were still supporting a system of secret banning and cutting of movies on a scale unprecedented anywhere in Europe outside the Communist bloc.

It was absurd to talk constructively about making movies in a country so busy repressing them.

Confessions of A Sewer Rat

The author posing for a mock photograph for
The Sunday Independent *after being repeatedly denounced for*
wallowing his way through filth and rubbish.

A selection of the author's books seized by Irish customs officials.

The author receiving the 1972 Showcase Award for cinema for his campaign against censorship. Harry Band of United Artists, who supplied a lot of inside information for the campaign, is to the left of the author.

John Boorman

Neil Jordan (staring into camera) with the novelist John McGahern to his right and the painter Theo McNab to his left.

Stephen Rea in Neil Jordan's **Angel.**

Ciaran Carty

Pat Murphy

*Brid Brennan in Pat Murphy's film **Anne Devlin**.*

Confessions of A Sewer Rat

Thaddeus O'Sullivan

Pat O'Connor

Ian McElhinney and Carol Scanlan in Joe Comerford's
Reefer and the Model.

Joe Comerford

Jim Sheridan

*Gabriel Byrne as Papa Riley in **Into the West**.*

Ciaran Carty

Brenda Fricker as Mrs Brown and Daniel Day Lewis as Christy Brown in My Left Foot.

Brendan Coyle in Paddy Breathnach's Ailsa, written by Joseph O'Connor

3

Is There A Doctor In The House?

It would be unfair to say that sixty-three-year-old general practitioner Dr Christopher Macken knew nothing about cinema when he was appointed Film Censor by Charles Haughey in April 1964.

Several years before he had actually been employed by 20th Century Fox when some scenes for the Henry King epic *Untamed* needed to be shot on location at Glencree, in the Dublin mountains.

Admittedly it was only for a week. But it did bring him into what could be called intimate contact with Susan Hayward. Her role as an Irish girl who falls in love with Dutch adventurer Tyrone Power on the great Boer trek required a lot of horse riding. Although an expert horsewoman, Hayward was not accustomed to riding sidesaddle, as was required of ladies in that period. Through having to use a leg rest she developed bursitis, otherwise known as 'housemaid's knee'. Dr Macken's job was to give her regular injections of penicillin in the bottom.

It turned out to be qualification enough when the sudden death of Liam O Hora gave Haughey a chance to place a Fianna Fail party faithful in the office of Film Censor. Having contested the 1948 elections as a candidate for Clann na Poblachta, Macken changed sides to stand for Fianna Fail in Dublin North West in 1954, only to receive the lowest vote of any candidate. Haughey suffered the same indignity in the adjoining North East constituency. Macken stood again in 1957, but was defeated for the last seat by Declan Costello.

Macken seemed to regard movies as some form of disease in need of ever-vigilant medical treatment, like smallpox or syphilis. "I suppose I have a better understanding of human nature due to my medical career," he said. "I took a postgraduate course in psychiatry about ten years ago in St Brendan's Hospital, Grangegorman, where I worked for about five years."

He admitted to liking good war movies. "My favourite picture in recent years was *The Longest Day*. I like films which teach a lesson, films that point to what could happen and what happened."

His appointment may have been a reward for loyal political service, but Haughey also had in mind an easing of Ireland's notoriously repressive film censorship. Since the Act setting up the system was passed in 1923 — the urgency with which it was regarded indicated by the fact that it was one of the Free State's first legislative decisions — around 2,300 movies had been banned and nearly 6,000 cut.

Democracy to the men of 1916 had meant freedom from British rule. It meant freedom to be Irish and Catholic. Having won this freedom, they didn't intend to have it undermined by subversive alien culture. Foreign games, foreign ideas, foreign beliefs were suspect in the Free State. School children were nurtured on the ideal of De Valera's comely maidens dancing at the crossroads (as articulated in his famous 1943 St Patrick's Day broadcast).

To the generation that followed, increasingly frustrated by the archaic narrow-minded strictures of an *as Gaelige* confessional state, this intolerant, nationalistic version of democracy seemed a ridiculous contradiction. If democracy was about anything in the 1960s, when even the church was prepared to entertain the concept of individual conscience at Vatican, it was about personal freedom.

When Haughey's successor, Brian Lenihan, revamped the Censorship of Film Appeals Board in 1965, replacing the ageing Senator JT O'Farrell, who had been chairman since 1929, and instituting a new policy of large-scale issuing of Limited Certificates, there was no opposition. It seemed that Irish audiences were belatedly deemed to have grown up.

What Lenihan hadn't allowed for was the dismantling of the notorious Hays Production Code in the US and the liberalisation of censorship in the UK under hitherto conservative British Board of Film Control secretary, John Trevelyan. Mainstream Hollywood and British movies were becoming progressively freer and more provocative, both in their themes and treatment. Explicit sex and violence were no longer taboo.

It was all a little too much for Dr Macken. While dutifully following the new guidelines on issuing limited certificates, he almost doubled the percentage of movies banned in 1965.

Initially this was not apparent. Censorship was conducted in secret. No details were issued on the Censor's decisions. For a time after 1965 it seemed to the public that movies were indeed getting through in their original form. Laurence Harvey's *The Ceremony* was shown with an uncut nude sequence showing Sarah Miles getting into bed with a lover. The lesbian theme of Lillian Hellman's *The Whisperers* wasn't watered down. Nor were the beatnik orgies of *The Party's Over*. Even *Room At the Top*, banned eight years before, suddenly seemed acceptable.

There were obvious absurdities, of course. The Appeals Board clamped Over 21 certificates on *Who's Afraid of Virginia Woolf* and *Alfie*, both of which were also cut. It seemed that while moviegoers at eighteen were deemed old enough to vote, marry or fight for their country, they were still too immature to be exposed to certain images on the screen.

Yet it was surely a sign of the times that Judge Conor Maguire, new chairman of the Appeals Board, came out into the open to answer my criticism in the *Sunday Independent* of his board's decision on *Who's Afraid Of Virginia Woolf.* "In restricting the exhibition of the film to persons Over 21, the Board took into account the nature of the theme, the violence of the emotions displayed, and the harshness of the language employed," he informed me. "The cuts were just a little shorter than you report: they were minimal — but necessary — and were not entirely dialogue cuts. They represent but some ten seconds out of a film of over two hours running time. They were done as unobtrusively as possible and did not affect either the continuity or essence of the film."

Up to then I'd made a practice of publishing the running times of movies I reviewed, as provided on the official studio synopsis. Now I began timing each movie to discover the actually running time in the cinema. I discovered that several minutes were missing from Alain Resnais's *The War Is Over*. Similarly with John Schlesinger's *A Kind Of Loving* (which no doubt explained the oddity of June Ritchie suddenly having a baby although none of her scenes with boyfriend Alan Bates contained any suggestion that they had sex together). Perhaps worst of all, at least three minutes were missing from Ingmar Bergman's meticulously edited masterpiece *Persona*. All three movies had originally been rejected by the Censor and came via the Appeals Board with Over 18 certificates. The cuts made a mockery of the policy introduced by Lenihan of widening the use of Over 18 certificates in order to make adult movies available to adult audiences.

My activities with a stopwatch proved too much for some readers. Hector Legge began receiving letters denouncing me as "a sewer rat wallowing in film filth" and "a Dublin 4 degenerate." A father of two castigated me for "polluting family life with continental obscenity": oddly, I had just become a father of two myself with the birth of our daughter, Estefania. A reader in Kerry branded me as "antiChrist" and threatened to strike me down. Heavy breathers began ringing Julia on Saturday nights (having discovered that I was at work at the *Independent* until 4 a.m., seeing the paper to press).

A more weighty response came from Father S Tiernan, a Catholic curate in Ballymote, Co Sligo. "Your film critic, Mr Ciaran Carty, seems to have a fixation about the little snippets removed by our censor and Appeals Board from some films. Sunday after Sunday, if he does not repeat his well-worn homily on the evils of censorship, he tells us with stop-watch accuracy how much we are missing from some masterpiece or other — usually either Swedish or Japanese.

"For my own part I am grateful to our censor for removing these embarrassing bits of dirt from otherwise good films, just as I thank my victualler when he trims off unwanted, unappetising bits from my steak before he sells it to me.

"I hate to see a genuine work of art sell itself to the prurient voyeur by inserting scenes totally unnecessary to the plot, and useful only for providing those 'daring' stills which help to draw the crowd. And what a crowd! I have so often seen these sad people queuing outside the 'art' cinemas of London and New York, pimply youths, middle-aged men with coat collars furtively turned up and hat brims down, a handful of pale bearded students and a scattering of lonely immigrants from warmer climes, all of whom have as much interest in art as a cat has in the laws of thermoydynamics.

"Strange how few women are interested in 'art'! Is anyone naive enough to believe that *I Am Curious Yellow* has run so long because of the sociological questionnaire that runs through it? Or that *Hair* is booked months in advance because of the patrons love of Rock Music? The old barker in the strip-club was at least honest when he announced, "Yes, sir, it's all for Art's sake, and if Art's in the front row I hope he enjoys it!

"May I repeat. I consider that our censor — himself a man of impeccable taste — is paying a compliment to our good taste in assuming that we would prefer not to see this filth.

"However, as Mr Carty seems so anxious about these gems being lost, I suggest he drop in to Harcourt Terrace and I daresay the censor would let him rescue them from the trash can. As they are all tediously alike, I'm sure they could be spliced together to form an artistic whole which Mr Carty could then show to art lovers who mourn their loss.

"I think he might be surprised to find how few would come to the party, and I feel certain that a man of his obvious talent and sincerity could well be ashamed of the company in which he found himself."

4

Not In Front Of The Children

I hadn't set out to take on the film censors. Initially I'd thought that a genuine policy of liberalising censorship had been initiated by the reforms introduced in 1965. But by 1969 it had become clear from viewing movies week after week that this liberalisation had been abandoned.

There was a suspicion that the Film Censor, Dr Macken, was responding to lobbying by the Catholic hierarchy and Catholic pressure groups. Letters from self-styled "Catholic laymen" began appearing in newspapers expressing concern at what was described as the "licentiousness that had become commonplace on Dublin cinema screens." *Mondo Bizarre, Our Kinky World* and *The Sweet Body of Deborah* were among movies cited as examples of "an objectionable permissive trend". The Archbishop of Dublin, Dr John Charles McQuaid, warned of the danger of films that "provoke sensuality".

"It is to be deplored," he wrote in his 1969 Lenten Regulations, "that following the licentious example of people who have rejected God and Christianity some publications, films and stage plays were lending their aid to the provocation of sensuality in thought and action."

My contacts with film distributors indicated that the number of movies being rejected by the Film Censor had increased and that there was a backlog of movies awaiting decision by the Appeals Board. One cinema manager told me: "Because of the *Mondo Bizarres* — which you can throw in the Liffey as far as

I am concerned— serious movies which should be showing here are running into difficulties."

Among movies named by my sources as experiencing delays of one kind or another were Lindsay Anderson's *If..., The Lion In Winter* (which had been filmed in Ireland and had won an Oscar for Katharine Hepburn), *The Prime of Miss Jean Brodie* (the 1969 Royal Command Performance choice), *Isadora* and *Rosemary's Baby.*

Some cinemas said that they were experiencing difficulty in finalising their programme arrangements and were obliged to screen stop-gap movies in place of those under consideration by the censorship authorities.

Yet my initial attempts to check out what was really happening ran up against a wall of silence. Annual statistics released by the Film Censor's Office were the only information available on the subject. These revealed that the previous year 652 movies were presented for censorship, 57 were passed with cuts and 35 rejected. Thirty-two went to the Appeals Board, of which only ten were rejected. No details were given about movies rejected or cuts made.

In the hope of getting more detailed information, I approached the Minister for Justice, who had responsibility for the Film Censor's Office and the Appeals Board. My request for details about films rejected and cut was turned down. "The Minister for Justice," I was informed, "has always felt precluded, on the grounds that it would involve a breach of confidence, from disclosing information about films submitted for censorship. Accordingly, even if the information you seek were available—and some of it is not — it would not be possible to give it to you.

"As far as the Minister for Justice and the Censor are concerned, information relating to identifiable films can be released to third parties only by the trade interests concerned."

The "trade interests concerned", of course, were naturally reluctant to jeopardise future negotiations with the Censor by revealing what went on during screenings in his office at Harcourt Terrace, and even if they were willing to talk freely, it would be difficult to gather together all the information needed to provide any kind of reliable overall picture.

This secretiveness compared oddly with the way the Censorship of Publications Board operated. As I had found out, their records were freely open to public scrutiny.

There seemed to be no legal justification for the double standards applying between books and movies. Neither the Censorship of Films Act 1923 nor the Amendments of 1925 and 1930 said anything about withholding information from the public.

My attack on this policy of secrecy was published as the main leader page article in the *Sunday Independent* on 4 May 1969: "Democratic self-government is based on a belief in the capacity of individuals to share in community decisions. Fundamental to this process is a properly informed public. Yet in the vital area of film censorship this public is not informed. It is deliberately kept in the dark by order of the Minister for Justice."

I pointed out that while the main justification for censorship was that it protected young people from harmful influences they might lack the maturity to withstand, too often film censorship was directed towards protecting adults. Movies like *Who's Afraid Of Virginia Woolf* and *Alfie* had been given Over 21 certificates. Movies with Over 18 certs, such as *The Graduate*, seemed to be cut as a matter of routine.

In the absence of information, it was difficult to discover what standards were being applied in protecting the public from themselves. Distributors submitting movies claimed that they had no idea what the Censor or the Appeals Board meant by obscenity. Shots passed in one movie might be cut in another. There was no consistency other than to treat every movie with suspicion.

The article flushed Dr Macken out of his lair. His response was to write a quasi-legal threatening letter to Hector Legge demanding retractions and apologies. My statement that film distributors were afraid to divulge information in case it might jeopardise future censorship negotiations was a "serious reflection" on him: "It goes without saying that a Censor who would behave in such a way would be unfit to be Censor."

He stated that the Film Renters Association had been formally consulted on his behalf after the article and had confirmed that they regarded the information sought by me as confidential information which the Censor should not disclose. "They are of course aware that I have not the slightest objection to their disclosing details of my decisions in relation to their films if they so desire."

Macken also denied that any films were awaiting censorship by him or that there was any backlog of films at the Appeals Board.

He concluded: "I now invite you to publish (1) an unqualified retraction of these false charges, and (2) an unqualified apology of such a nature as will undo, insofar as any apology now made can undo, the injury that has been done to me."

Hector Legge had no intention of issuing any retraction. He didn't even show Macken's letter to our lawyers. All he suggested was that in attacking censorship I keep the focus on the system rather than on the actual individuals, like Macken, who were charged with implementing it.

We published Macken's letter in full, with a response in which I said that I was "sorry Dr Macken sees in my articles a serious reflection on himself personally...the purpose of the articles was to criticise the system of film censorship in Ireland as a whole, not the people who perform the difficult and onerous task of making it work."

I picked up on his denial that he was responsible for any secrecy, saying that "I welcome Dr Macken's statement that he has not the slightest objection to renters disclosing details of his decisions in relation to their films if they so desire. This is a progressive attitude which should help the growth of useful debate on what kind of censorship is best for the Irish."

As it turned out, this remark by Macken was to provide me with the weapon that would bring about his downfall and the collapse of the repressive system he had come to epitomise.

5

Excessive And Lustful Kissing

The Censorship of Films Act was introduced in 1923 by Minister for Home Affairs, Kevin O'Higgins, almost before the last shots had been fired in the Civil War. Until then censorship had been the responsibility of local authorities. In 1922 Dublin Corporation's Public Health Committee appointed twenty-two censors (six to be nominated by the Catholic and Protestant Archbishops), an unwieldly system which collapsed in chaos.

Dublin Corporation, together with such diverse bodies as the Priest Social Guild and the Irish Vigilance Association then lobbied O'Higgins to intervene. Under the O'Higgins Act, which still applies, the Censor was required to withhold certificates from any films he deemed to be "indecent, blasphemous or obscene". The Act didn't specify any qualifications for the job and it would seem that none were thought necessary by the Department of Justice because, in the absence due to holidays or illness of the Censor and his Deputy, ordinary officials from the Department could take over the work.

Yet the Censor's responsibilty, as set out, was even more demanding than that of a judge since he had only his own subjective judgement to guide him in deciding which movies or parts thereof might be likely "to inculcate principles contrary to public morality or would be otherwise subversive of public morality."

Yet the office was to be operated over the years as if it were as uncontroversial and as automatic as a dog-licensing authority.

The first Censor James Montgomery, on being asked what he knew about movies, replied: "Nothing, but I know the Ten Commandments." Both Montgomery, who was in office from 1 November 1923 to 31 October 1940, and his successor, Dr Richard Hayes, had scholarly work to their credit. Montgomery, whose son Niall became a well known architect and Joycean expert, had published research on Irishmen in France in the eighteenth-century; Hayes was an authority on the diarist Joseph Holloway.

The suspicion that the authorities regarded movies as some sort of disease was confirmed when Dr Martin Brennan succeeded Dr Hayes in January 1954. A hunger striker who had been prominent in the War of Independence, he served in the Dail from 1938-48 as Fianna Fail Deputy for Sligo. He had assisted Professor Delargy in the collection of folklore in the West of Ireland and undertaken research in philology and Irish dialect with Professor O Maille in Galway. His appointment, it seemed, was a reward for a lifetime of loyal service to Fianna Fail.

On his death two years later, forty-year-old Liam O Hora, father of eleven, became the youngest Irish Censor ever. A first cousin of the Bishop of Down and Connor, Dr Philbin, and brother of Father Cormac of Mount Argus, he'd served in the Palestine Police during World War II, returning in 1948 to become manager of the Gaiety Theatre. He was called to the Bar in 1954.

Until Dr Macken's appointment in 1964, nearly all the movies submitted to the Irish Censor had already been subjected to stringent preproduction vetting in the UK and the US. His misfortune was to take up office at a time when virtually all restrictions were being lifted from movies. A new wave of auteur directors was suddenly free to confront challenging issues and depict every form of human behaviour in the most explicit manner and using the most frank language. By the end of the 1960s, virtually no limits remained in Western cinema.

Following a series of scandals in Hollywood in the early silent days, the American industry had decided to clean up its act itself rather than be cleaned up by outsiders. Will H Hays, a former lawyer and chairman of the Republican National Committee, and US Postmaster General in President Harding's cabinet, was head-hunted by the studio moguls to run their new Motion Picture Producers and Distributors of America organisation (MPPDA). By 1930 he had devised a self-regulatory charter of do's and don't's that became known as the Hays Code. It came fully into effect in 1934 and was to remain virtually unchanged until 1966.

The Hays Code's paternalistic guiding principle was that no movie should be produced that would "lower the standards of those who see it. Hence the sympathy of the audience should never be thrown on the side of crime, wrongdoing, evil or sin." To achieve this, an astonishing array of specifics were drawn up. "Miscegenation (sex relationships between white and black races) is forbidden"; "the sanctity of the institution of marriage and the home shall be upheld"; "excessive and lustful kissing, lustful embracing, suggestive postures and gestures, are not to be shown...indecent or undue exposure is forbidden...sex perversion or any inference to it is forbidden".

Bedroom scenes were prohibited from showing characters in bed together: they always had to have at least one foot on the ground. This resulted in the practice of using single instead of double beds: according to Ronald Reagan, this then became a popular fashion, moviegoers copying it because they thought it must be sophisticated since they'd seen it in the movies.

Any movie that failed to comply with the Hays Code was denied a seal of approval, which automatically excluded it from most American cinemas. Few producers dared to challenge the system until the 1960s, when a series of civil liberties test cases and Supreme Court rulings led to a total overhaul of the Code in 1966. A rating system was put into effect in 1968.

In the UK most producers submitted scripts to the British Board of Film Control before production began. The Board would often make detailed suggestions which the producers were expected to implement: if they didn't, the Board would almost certainly enforce them more damagingly on the finished movie. To avoid interference, director Stanley Kubrick himself pre-empted the British censors and the Motion Picture Association of America by raising the age of Vladamir Nabokov's nymphet heroine in *Lolita* from twelve to fourteen.

By 1964 John Trevelyan, secretary of the British Board of Film had come to the conclusion that changing attitudes and the greater openness in society were making the concept of censorship redundant. "The British Board of Film Censors cannot assume responsibility for the guardianship of morality. It cannot refuse for exhibition to adults, films that show behaviour which contravanes the accepted moral code, and it does not demand that 'the wicked' should always be punished. It cannot legitimately refuse to pass films which criticize 'the Establishment' and films which express minority opinions." Accordingly he was prepared to allow pubic hair in Lindsay Anderson's *If...* in 1967, and a nude wrestling scene between Oliver Reed and Alan Bates in Ken Russell's *Women In Love* in 1969.

By the end of the 1960s the full impact of this permissiveness was becoming evident in the movies being submitted for censorship in Ireland. Dr Macken panicked, banning sixty-eight movies in 1969 compared with thirty-four in 1968. Thirty-six of these bannings were upheld by the Appeals Board.

Macken's obsession was with sex, blasphemy and crude language: violent scenes were rarely cut or banned. During 1969, my research revealed that five minutes had been cut from Paul Newman's *Rachel, Rachel*, two minutes from *If...*, nearly a minute from Truffaut's *Stolen Kisses*, and ten minutes from *The Private Right*. Polanski's *Rosemary's Baby* was rejected altogether, as were *Hard Contract, I Love You Alice B Toklas*, and *Les Biches*. More alarming, by the end of the year up to twenty movies were experiencing difficulties, including *Women In Love* and *Midnight Cowboy* (whose producers were refusing to accept cuts demanded by the Appeals Board).

This inability of Irish censorship to adapt to the 1960s was brought to a head in a bizarre way on the eve of the 1969 Cork Film Festival. Two letters were received by the Festival organisers from the Roman Catholic Bishop of Cork, Dr Lucey, urging the withdrawal of the gala opening movie *I Can't I Can't*, which had been filmed at Ardmore Studios and dealt with contraception in contemporary Ireland. The Bishop objected to the movie on the grounds that it contained nude scenes which, he claimed, would lead to immodest thoughts, looks and words from many people and in any case could not but be offensive to decency and good taste. He stressed that the festival authorities were bound in conscience and decency to try to prevent the movie from being shown.

At a hastily assembled emergency meeting, the Festival council under the chairmanship of former Lord Mayor Gus Healy, courageously stuck to their guns. The movie was screened as programmed. Opening the Festival, Frank O'Reilly, chairman of the cigarette company Player Wills, who were co-promoters with Bord Failte, went onto the attack. He claimed that appreciation of movies as an art form would have made much greater progress in Ireland, were it not for existing censorship. "I acknowledge the need for censorship," he said, "but I think there is room for improvement in our present system." He called for a more realistic grading system, and said that it seemed strange that mature audiences should be denied the opportunity of seeing many fine artistic works in their entirety, or at all, because of censorship.

On Monday morning Bishop Lucey retaliated in a statement criticising the festival for showing *I Can't I Can't* against his advice. He also defended the censorship system. "The blind assumption that anything cut by the censor is of artistic value is utter nonsense," he said. He added that he thought it impertinent of commercial people advertising themselves to lecture the public on good taste and censorship.

O'Reilly was one of the few public figures in Ireland to speak out on the record against censorship. Nearly everyone I talked to in Cork agreed with what he had said, but many felt that he had spoken at the wrong time and in the wrong context. Dermot Breen, the Cork public relations man who had started the Festival in 1956 as a way of promoting tourism and was its programme director, was similarly cagey when I confronted him.

"Do you agree with what Mr O'Reilly said?" I asked.

"I agree with everything Mr O'Reilly said about the need for censorship," he said.

"Do you feel that the present system could be improved?"

"Yes. The emphasis is too much on sex and not enough on violence. You know, we are by no means the only country with censorship. It is much more stringent in South America and certain European countries."

Putting forward the practices of banana republic dictatorships and Stalinist regimes as a measure for Irish censorship seemed strange, but as a public relations man Breen was adept at covering his real opinions in language acceptable to the Establishment.

Our conversation, a rehearsal for many more to come when he himself would succeed Dr Macken as censor, continued on these surreal lines.

"Would you agree that Irish film censorship has improved in recent years?"

"Well, I hear fewer complaints from film people I meet abroad. You could call that an improvement if you like."

"But many important movies are still being cut or rejected?"

"Yes. Very often films that are rejected are not worth anything at all. I think that the present system of censorship is too much of a burden on the Censor. It is asking too much of any man to arbitrate on every film. The Appeals Board shows what group censorship can achieve."

Breen spoke enthusiastically about the idea of a get-together of people concerned about movies to try to devise terms of reference on censorship. I took up the idea in the *Sunday Independent* in a leader page article, calling for a Government-appointed commission or committee of inquiry into the whole issue of censorship. It could study how movies affect people of different ages and emotional backgrounds and define exactly what was meant by obscenity and pornography as applied to movies.

Its brief would be to devise effective ways of safeguarding children without sacrificing art or condemning adults to sanitised cinema.

Nothing came of the proposal.

Soon after I found myself attempting to review *The Private Right* at the International Film Theatre. It was a film about the Cyprus troubles by a promising young director, Michael Papas. Ten minutes had been cut from it by the Appeals Board. The opening sequence, showing a running battle between British troopd and EOKA fighters, was a model of economy and showed how an authentic feeling of tension and excitement could be created by unexaggerated use of a hand-held camera. Elsewhere there was a tendency to indulge in virtuosity for virtuosity's sake — perhaps inevitable in a first movie — and the nightmare finale verged on pretentiousness. Yet it would have been unfair to review it in its mutilated condition. I found it impossible to pass judgement on a movie that had had its core removed.

By now this had become an almost weekly experience. Irish censorship was not going to reform itself. The only way to bring about change was through a persistent campaign of exposure and ridicule.

CHAPTER THREE

WHAT THE CENSOR SAW BUT DIDN'T WANT TO SAY

A deranged Glenda Jackson, shaven and filthy, squats over the grating covering the cells in a Tsarist Russian lunatic asylum and allows the inmates below to fondle her...

Never, said Dr Christopher Macken — and banned Ken Russell's extravagantly imagined Tchaikovsky biopic *The Music Lovers*.

Banned too in 1970 by Ireland's Censor was the maverick Yugoslav director Dusan Makavejev's anarchic *Diary Of The Switchboard Operator*, one presumes for showing pubic hair. Similarly Pier Paolo Pasolini's *Theorem*, for the male variation, a fleeting glimpse of Terence Stamp's penis.

There was nothing so explicit in Ingmar Bergman's *The Rite* or *A Passion*. It's possible the local parallels in *The Rite* were just too close for comfort. A famous theatrical troupe have their act stopped in a provincial town because it is considered obscene. Called before an examining judge, their private lives and neuroses are ruthlessly exposed: the implication is that because their morals are unconventional, their work is automatically suspect.

Bergman's movies — the work of a Swedish atheist notorious for his affairs with his actresses — were similarly stigmatised by Macken. Indeed his harsh and incomprehensible treatment in 1968 of *Persona*, arguably one of the masterpieces of contemporary cinema, from which he excised seven minutes (an action which the Appeals Board supported), had been one of the actions which first alerted me to the fact that the so-called reform of film censorship was turning out to be a sham.

Violence didn't often trouble Dr Macken, but the slow motion blood-bath in Sam Peckinpah's classic western *The Wild Bunch* proved too much. Or perhaps the fact that it could also be read as an allegory for Vietnam, and therefore anti-American?

With Mike Nichols's faithful adaptation of Joseph Heller's irreverent anti-war satire *Catch 22* and Robert Altman's similarly anti-establishment *MASH*, he apparently couldn't tolerate the uninhibitedly frank dialogue.

Whatever the reasons, the repressive treatment of these and other movies made any pretence of providing the public with a critical appraisal of what was relevent in contemporary cinema seem to me to be a hypocritical charade. Even worse, by continuing to function week after week as a critic I was in effect collaborating with the system. At the very least the public had a right to be informed about what was being done allegedly on their behalf.

From talking with various distributors, who by now had grown to trust me, it was clear that their dissatisfaction with the system was nearing the breaking point too. The Censorship Of Films (Amendment) Act, which in 1970 introduced a "seven-year rule" whereby films banned or cut could be resubmitted after a period of seven years, was unlikely to be improve the situation, given the Censor's hostility to movies.

Dr Macken was probably bluffing when he claimed, in his threatening letter to the *Sunday Independent* the previous year, that he had not "the slightest objection" to film renters disclosing details of his decisions in relation to their films. He was bargaining on the fact that while one or two renters might leak information with regard to particular movies, it would be impossible to get them all to agree to provide the kind of detailed information on a regular basis that would be necessary to monitor what was going on behind the closed doors of Harcourt Terrace. It was time to call his bluff.

Harry Band, manager of United Artists, was the first distributor I approached. An East Londoner with a ribald sense of humour, he'd been one of the first Jewish settlers to go to the newly independent Israel in 1947. Although in his forties, he'd tried to volunteer again when the Six Day War broke out in 1967. He readily agreed to act as a Deep Throat, confidentially feeding me information on all censorship decisions relating to UA movies for a monthly black-list of banned and cut movies that I proposed to publish.

Twentieth-Century Fox's Gerry Duffy, who was particularly perceptive on the new American cinema, having alerted me to Bob Rafelson's promising feature debut *Head*, followed Band's lead. Gerry Crofton at Columbia and Dermot O'Sullivan at Ranks were cooperative too. The independent distributor Michael Collins was meanwhile already leaking me information.

But before launching the black-list it seemed only fair to give Dr Macken one more chance. I rang up his office and asked if they could confirm whether cuts had been made in *Catch 22*.

"I'm sorry. That information belongs to the film renters. I cannot tell you."

The first monthly black-list of banned and cut movies was published in the *Sunday Independent* on 31 January 1971. It launched a campaign that within two years successfully undermined the working of the censorship system and resulted in the appointment of Dermot Breen to succeed Macken as Censor. Breen's first act as Censor was to agree to being interviewed by me at his office in Harcourt Terrace. An era of openness and liberalisation was inaugurated which slowly but inexorably brought about a virtual end to the cutting and banning of movies: by the 1980s the censor had become in effect not a censor as such but merely a granter of certificates regulating the audience suitability of movies. Meanwhile the bizarre ups and downs of this campaign of public ridicule are perhaps best captured in the form of a public diary.

31 January 1971

The black-list ("compiled without official cooperation") is launched with a photograph of Silvana Mangano in Pasolini's banned *Theorem*. The list promises to be "as accurate and complete as difficult circumstances permit."

Publication of a monthly list of film censorship decisions is merely following the example of the Censorship of Publication Board, which each month provides newspapers with a list of prohibited books and magazines. Why should there be one law for books and another for film?

The fundamental point is that information about censorship decisions is not the property of the Minister for Justice, the Censor or the film renters: it belongs to the public and should be freely available to them. The state has taken upon itself the right to censor movies on behalf of the public, yet it totally disregards the corresponding obligation to provide the public with the

---

The January 1971 List

- Censorship of movies screened in Dublin first-run cinemas in January 1971: *Borsalino* (over 16, no cuts), *The Secret of Santa Vittoria* (over 18, no cuts), *A Passion* (Over 18, several cuts), *Waterloo* (no cuts), *Darling Lili* (no cuts), *Catch 22* (Appeals Board, Over 18, several cuts), *The Railway Children* (no cuts), *Night Of The Living Dead* (Appeals Board, Over 18, cuts), *Rio Lobo* (no cuts), *Tora, Tora, Tora* (no cuts), *El Condor* (Over 16, several cuts), *Irma La Douce* (Over 18, no cuts), *The Boatniks* (no cuts), *Anne of a Thousand Days* (Over 12, no cuts), *Scrooge* (no cuts), *The April Fools* (Over 12 no cuts), *The Guru* (over 16, no cuts), *The Honeymoon Killers* (over 18, cuts)

- Films with the Appeals Board, following rejection by the censor: *The Rite, The Music Lovers, Satyricon, MASH, Leo The Last, Entertaining Mr Sloane, Diary of the Switchboard Operator, What Do You Do With A Naked Lady?*

- Films banned: *Theorem, Bob and Carol, Ted And Alice, Goodbye Columbus, Love is a Splendid Illusion, Benjamin, The Wild Bunch*

information necessary to access whether that right is being correctly exercised. As a result, moviegoers are paying money in good faith at the box-office for what may well be a butchered version of the advertised movie. At the very least, this is an infringement of fair trade practice.

21 February 1971

Lent is a time when the Church rallies the faithful. Should the Censor waver in application of Catholic morality to popular cinema, Dr John Charles McQuaid, the Roman Catholic Archbishop of Dublin, is on hand this morning to remind him of his duty. The Lenten Pastorals and Regulations of the Hierarchy are always published in full by Irish newspapers. Conor O'Brien, who succeeded Hector Legge as editor last autumn, agrees to me breaking with tradition by giving His Grace's admonitions a more selective and critical treatment. The idea is to intercut italicised quotations with editorial asides. Irreverent, perhaps, but a way to expose how paternalistic Church attitudes underpin film censorship.

"Lent can be a disillusioning time for those of us who work with words and image. Invariably Dr John Charles McQuaid utters dire warnings about the evils of our profession," I wrote.

"Occasions of sin are being multiplied by the means of communication. Our Divine Lord, who is truth itself, has given us an unfailing standard by which to judge: 'By their fruits you will know them' *(Matt. V 1618). Books, newspapers, magazines, films, television features, especially stage plays, of necessity reveal the vulgarity or nobility of the authors and actors, directors and producers.*"

"How does one quantify occasions of sin? Were there more occasion of sin last year than the year before? Is the world less pure now than 100 years ago, when there were no movies, no television sets and no mass circulation newspapers? Since danger so obviously lurks in the means of communication, is one to conclude that the safest state for faith and morals is a world of hermits totally without human intercourse, where each person exists in intellectual and sensual isolation, uncontaminated by any influence other than one's self?"

"If men or women be unjust, their words and actions will be unjust. If they are uncharitable, they will belittle or subtly defame the object of their dislikes. If they are cruel, they will use their power to crush the lowly who cannot defend themselves. If they are sensual, they will search for anything that can stimulate themselves and others to unchaste imaginations and unlawful satisfaction. If, in addition, they are cowardly, they will have recourse to the slinking refuge of anonymous publication. And, what is worst of all, if they be themselves in error concerning the Faith, they will spread confusion, under the cover of so-called humanism, or even so-called renewal of Catholic life."

"Is a newspaper or a play or a book or a film morally corrupt and corrupting if the people who create it do not conform to Catholic morality? If artists are less than perfect as human beings or in their relationships, does that invalidate their art? How much art could survive such a stringent test?"

"What a fruitful cooperation with the grace of Our Divine Redeemer the means of communication could achieve in the modern world if only the masters who give themselves the vocation to mould could instead keep constantly in mind the admonition of the Holy Spirit: 'Whatever is true, whatever is lovely, whatever is pure, whatever is gracious, if there is any excellence, if there is anything worthy of praise, think about these.' *(Philippians V, 8)."*

"Are you listening, Dr Macken? And would it not be charitable to concede that perhaps those who are responsible for the means of communication, whatever their shortcomings, might not also be inspired by such ideals? That goodness is not the monopoly of the moralists? That the artist, no matter how flawed as a person, might nevertheless still strive to achieve truth and beauty through art?"

28 February 1971

The pattern of movies on the banned list this month suggests that no matter what the treatment, any movie dealing with irregular sexual relationships outside marriage is liable to be rejected by Dr Macken.

Dustin Hoffman and Mia Farrow have a one-night fling in *John And Mary*, then toy with the idea of staying together. In *Joanna*, an art student comes up to London from the provinces and is taken advantage of by a variety of predatory males.

John And Mary, by Bullitt director Peter Yates, is a thoughtful and wryly perceptive reflection on the pressures of contemporary mores; *Joanna* is a pathetically inept and poorly acted soap opera. To the Censor they are no different: their theme by its very nature is considered subversive to public morality.

Similarly *Last Summer* (sexual adventures of teenagers at summer seaside holiday resort), written by Eleanor Perry and directed by her husband Frank Perry, and *Three In the Attic* starring Barbara Hershey (college girls abduct campus Don Juan and give him taste of his own medicine until he begs for mercy) also run foul of the Censor.

Hard Contract might have got by as a tough thriller: its mistake was to give hit-man James Coburn sexual hang-ups which he tries to confront.

The Appeals Board has overturned the Censor's bans on Fellini's *Satyricon*, Bergman's *The Rite*, Russell's *The Music Lovers* and Makavjev's *Diary of the Switchboard Operator* only to pass them Over 18 with cuts. This seems to be the automatic fate of any important director: trash movies worry the Censor less — witness passing without cuts of *The Vampire Lovers*, a movie with no artistic claims but generous helpings of nipples and pubic hair — than movies with anything serious to say and the ability to say it with real feeling or conviction.

Never mind that it's restricted to Over 18s, the Censor has still removed over five minutes from Bo Widerburg's widely acclaimed *Adalen 31*, which deals with the bloody suppression of a strike by troops during the Depression. *Zabriskie Point*, Michelangelo Antonioni's brilliant parable on American anti-Vietnam War campus protest, has been similarly sanitised: Irish adults, it seems, lack the maturity to consider such issues.

Initial reader response to publication of the monthly black-list has been encouraging. Mr James Lynch of Fairview writes: "The moralistic stance of our censors is not simply one of holier-than-thou, but it appears to me on examination to be founded on the assumption (wrong, I suggest) that we, the cinema-going public, have minds as dirty as they (the censors) have." And Mr R Dunne of the South Circular Road writes: "Just a note to let you know you have plenty of support for your views on film censorship in this country."

19 March 1971

Harry Band rings to congratulate me on the birth of our second son, Antonio. Then the bad news: director John Schlesinger, after holding out for several months, has capitulated to pressure from United Artists in the US and agreed to allow his Academy Award winning *Midnight Cowboy* to be released in Ireland in the mutilated form demanded by the Appeals Board (three key sequences, crucial to an understanding of the relationship

---

The February 1971 List

- Censorship of movies screened in Dublin first-run cinemas in February 1971: *Adalen 31* (Over 18, cuts), *Sunflower* (Over 18), *Woodstock* (Over 16, dialogue cuts), *Heartbeat* (Appeals Board, Over 18, cuts), *The Reivers* (Over 16, no cuts), *The Vampire Lovers* (Over 18, no cuts), *Zabriskie Point* (Appeals Board, Over 18, cuts), *The Music Lovers* (Appeals Boards, Over 18, cuts), *The Adventures of Gerard* (Over 16, cuts), *How Do I Love Thee* (Over 18, no cuts)
- Under Appeal: *The Landlord, The Watermelon Man, The Buttercup Chain, Leo the Last, What Do You Do with A Naked Lady?*
- Banned: *The Body, Hard Contract, Last Summer, John And Mary, Three In the Attic, Joanna*

between sexual hustler Jon Voight, and Dustin Hoffman, the cantankerous drifter he takes up with, have been excised). Antonioni was similarly obliged to give way to contractual pressure and accept cuts in *Blow Up* two years ago. Even major directors, it seems, have little or no power to decide what happens with their work once it has been delivered to distributors.

April 4 1971

Censorship is justified on the basis that it protects Ireland from hardcore 'sexploitation' movies. Yet it is already clear from the monthly black-list that these movies rarely if ever come before the Censors. Virtually all the movies submitted for censorship are either mainstream or art-house entertainment. It is also clear that the main thrust of censorship decisions is directed towards suppressing or mutilating the work of universally respected and acclaimed directors: the hit list this year so far includes Schlesinger, Peckinpah, Visconti, Lean, Antonioni, Widerberg, Pasolini, Bergman and Mike Nichols.

The censorship system in its present form would seem to have developed into excessive intrusion by the State into the realms not only of art and entertainment but also of private morality. It has become in effect a tool of the Roman Catholic Hierarchy, regulating cinema according to what are assumed to be the moral beliefs and standards of the Roman Catholic majority. The Censor and the Appeals Board are sitting in moral judgement on every image and every word in every movie submitted to them. It's as absurd and intolerable as the State presuming to decide on moral grounds which parts of a Picasso painting are fit to be seen, or what paragraph of a Graham Greene novel ought to be excised.

The solution: impose limitations on the Censor's power to cut and ban movies. In the case of Over 18 movies, the Censor should only have the power to ban, not to cut. The essential criteria in reaching a decision on Over 18 movies should be the intent of the director and overall artistic merit of the movie rather than any possible moral considerations.

The power to cut movies would be retained only in the case of movies submitted for Under 18 certification. The criteria for these movies would be the potential effect of disturbing sequences on impressionable youngsters of various ages.

Under such a system, in which the Censor would primarily be concerned with grading movies, the public would know what to expect under each classification and would be protected, in so far as they wished to be, from material being thrust upon them that they might consider embarrassing or unsuitable. Renters and cinema managers would find their position improved. They would have a clear idea where they stood when they submitted movies for censorship.

The March 1971 List

- Censorship of movies in Dublin first-run cinemas in March 1971: *Ryan's Daughter* (Over 16, cuts), *Tick, Tick, Tick* (Over 16, cuts), *The Walking Stick* (Over 18, cuts), *The Wild Bunch* (Appeals Board, Over 16, cuts), *The Illustrated Man* (Over 16, no cuts), *You Can't Win 'Em All* (no cuts), *The Trials of Oscar Wilde* (Appeals Board, Over 16, no cuts), *The Damned* (Over 18, cuts), *The New Interns* (Over 12, no cuts), *Midnight Cowboy* (Appeals Board, Over 18, cuts), *Oedipus Rex* (Appeals Board, no cuts), *Two Mules for Sister Sara* (Over 16, no cuts), *Strangers When We Meet* (Over18, no cuts), *When Dinosaurs Ruled the Earth* (no cuts), *The Great Bank Robbery* (no cuts), *Night After Night After Night* (Over 18, cuts), *4 rode Out* (Over 18, no cuts), *The Candy Man* (Over 18, no cuts), *The Battle of Algiers* (Over 18, no cuts), *Fragments of Fear* (over 16, no cuts), *The Bargee* (Over 16, not cuts)

- Before the Appeals Board: *The Boys In the Band, My Lover My Son, Myra Brekinridge, The Buttercup Chain*

- Banned: *Cover Me Babe, Run Shadow Run, What Do You Do With A Naked Lady?*

2 May 1971

Conor O'Brien passes on some anonymous hate mail. "They're crying for your blood," he says. Complains Mentes Sanae from Dublin: "You cannot really desire that this kind of stuff should appear in your newspaper." Padraic O'Hara from Ballina demands to know "my qualifications, academic or otherwise as a film critic and as a moralist." He castigates "the tripe dished up in the name of art by innovating amoral theorists who are nothing short of sexmaniacs, or simply dirty ould men, people like Bunuel, Bergman and their ilk. Their works may be experiments with sex abuse, perversion or some such, but whatever they are please get this straight, Mr Carthy (sic), of the Irish name but the very unIrish mentality, we here in Ireland do not want to see them. So if you and a few more of the codded intelligentsia want to see such films as *Theorem*, I suggest you do the obvious — go over to Britain or to the continent where they have neither culture nor art nor moral standards."

Later in the day the porter in reception has some difficulty holding back a large red-faced man who tries to force his way upstairs to my office "to strike down the Anti-Christ."

A letter from Ms Rita Treacy in this context is reassuring. "Having recently emerged from the film *Midnight Cowboy* feeling bewildered and cheated, due to the severe cuts made by the Censor, I would like to say how much I agree with you on the issue of the present, most unsatisfactory form of censorship. I take this film as a prime example: there have been many, many more, treated in the same manner, as I'm sure you are well aware. I think a protest should be staged outside the Censor's office, and if such was arranged, I would certainly lend my support, as I'm sure would many others who share the some sentiments on the present state of censorship."

During April, my sources reveal that Fellini's *Satyricon* and Altman's *MASH* suffered the same fate as *Midnight Cowboy*: cleared by the Appeals Board but with Over 18 certs **and** cuts.

So why go on about a few minutes cut from a movie? Because how a movie is cut determines its whole meaning: editing is the essential grammar of cinema. Sidney Lumet, director of *Twelve Angry Men*, puts it succinctly: "The moment of a cut, the moment you physically slice a film, is as critical to the picture as the choice of lens, the lens opening, the placement of key lighting — too critical to be left to another mind. It a cut were changed in a movie of mine I think I would take my name off it: it's that important to me."

6 June 1971

A friend from Sweden enlightens me on the work of the Swedish Film Institute, which is financed by a ten percent levy on film admissions. It contains a library of over 20,000 movies and arranges screenings of creatively significant movies in centres throughout Sweden. It also subsidises film studies in schools and a supports a Chair of Cinema at the University of Stockholm.

It is humiliating to have to tell her that the State only involves itself in cinema in Ireland for the purposes of suppression. Its function is totally negative. No attempt has been made to introduce cinema appreciation courses in the schools. Cinema is

---

The April 1971 List

- Censorship of movies in Dublin first-run cinemas in April 1971: *Satyricon* (Appeals Board, Over 18, cuts), *Love Story* (Over 16 no cuts), *The Raging Moon* (Over 18, cut), *Hoffman* (Over 16, cuts), *Secret World* (Over 18, no cuts), *The Private Life of Sherlock Holmes* ((Over 16, no cuts), *Monte Walsh* (no cuts), *MASH* (Appeals Board, Over 18 cuts), *The Confession* (Over 18, no cuts) *When Eight Bells Toll* (no cuts), *The World of Suzie Wong* (Appeals Board, resubmitted 11 years after banning, Over 18, no cuts), *Danse Macabre* (Over 18, cuts)
- Under Appeal: *The Boys of the Band, My Lover My Son, Beyond the Valley of the Dolls, The Travelling Executioner, De Sade, The Queer And The Erotic*

ignored by the universities. The Arts Council, supposedly dedicated to the promotion of culture in Ireland, seems unaware of cinema's existence.

4 July 1971

The Appeals Board has upheld the Censor's banning of *The Boys From The Band*, the first Hollywood movie openly about homosexuals. A man who says he's not gay attends a party given by eight homosexuals — the idea is that each represents a different gay stereotype. Despite its negative attitude ("You show me a happy homosexual and I'll show you a dead corpse"), Mark Crowley's play performed to packed houses at Dublin's Olympia Theatre before Christmas. Yet the material, adapted by Crowley and directed by William Friedkin, is now deemed unsuitable for film audiences (no doubt in many cases the same people who saw it on the stage).

The May 1971 List

- Censorship of movies screened in Dublin first-run cinemas in May 1971: *Death In Venice* (Over 16, no cuts), *Entertaining Mr Sloane* (Appeals Board, Over 18, cuts), *The Mackenzie Break* (Over 16, cuts), *They Call Me Mr Tibbs* (Over18, no cuts), *Waiting For Caroline* (Appeals Board, Over 18, cuts), *The Cry of the Banshee* (Over18, no cuts), *Count Yorga Vampire* (Over 18 , no cuts), *The Christine Jorgensen Story* (Appeals Board, Over 18, cuts), *Where The Action Is* (Over 18, no cuts), *The Horrible Profession* (Over 18, no cuts), *Say Hello To Yesterday* (Over 18, no cuts), *Master of the Islands* (Over 16, no cuts), *Hornet's Nest* (no cuts), *The Landlord* (Appeals Board, Over 18, dialogue cuts), *AKA Cassius Clay* (Over 16, no cuts), *Underground* (no cuts), *Jealousy Italian Style* (Over 16, no cuts), T*he House That Dripped Bloo*d (Over 16, no cuts), *The Revolutionary* (Over 18, cuts), *Every Home Should Have One* (Over 18, no cuts)
- Under Appeal: *BS I Love You, The Boys Of The Band, Pussycat Pussycat I Love You, Beyond the Valley Of The Dolls, My Lover My Son*
- Banned: *The Queer and the Erotic*

Important directors continue to be targeted by the Censor. Pasolini's *Pigsty*, Gino Pontecorvo's *Queimada* and Bob Rafelson's *Five Easy Pieces* have all gone to appeal.

The monthly black-list shows that in the first six months of 1971, nineteen of 117 movies submitted have been banned and cuts were made in thirty-three (all either Over 16 or Over 18) of the ninety-nine passed.

None of this information was made available to the public by the Censor, despite a requirement in the Censorship of Films Act 1923 that when the Censor attaches restrictions to the screening of a movie, "he shall grant a certificate that such picture is fit for public exhibition subject to such restrictions and conditions (which shall be expressed on the certificate) in regard to the places at which or the special conditions under which the picture may be exhibited or the classes of persons who may be admitted."

The June 1971 List

- Censorship of movies in first-run Dublin cinemas in June: *Angels From Hell* (Over 16, cuts), *Eyewitness* (general, no cuts), *All The Way Home* (general, no cuts), *Soldier Blue* (Over 18, cuts), *The Music Lovers* (Appeals Board, Over 18, cuts), *The Man Who Had Power Over Women* (Appeals Board, Over 18, cuts), *The Long Day's Dying* (Appeals Board, Over 18, cuts), *Goodbye Again* (Appeals Board, resubmitted, Over 16, no cuts), *Fraulein Doktor* (Over 18, no cuts), *Bandits in Rome* (Over 18, no cuts), *There Was A Crooked Man* (Over 18, no cuts), *Assault* (Over 16, no cuts), *Loving* (Over 18, cuts), *Bronco Bullfrog* (general, no cuts)

- Under Appeal: *The Statue, Pigsty, Valdez Is Coming, Queimada, Pussycat Pussycat I Love you, BS I Love You, Five Easy Pieces, The Owl And the Pussycat*

- Banned: *Myra Breckinridge, My Lover My Son, Beyond the Valley Of the Dolls, The Boys Of The Band.*

30 July 1971

While the Film Censor was on holidays for the past two weeks, movies submitted to his office for certification were viewed by Ms S Ni Thuathaigh, a higher executive officer in the Department of Justice. Last year, Mr Denis Coakley, an assistant secretary in the Department, was similarly employed as a stopgap censor and banned Jiri Menzel's small masterpiece, *Closely Observed Trains*.

The Censorship of Films Act 1923 gives the Minister for Justice absolute power to appoint a film censor without requiring that the person appointed should have any experience or knowledge of cinema. Whenever the Censor is temporarily unavailable for whatever reason, the Minister can appoint anyone he chooses as deputy. Yet people so appointed are then given free rein to cut a movie in whatever way they deem appropriate if they are of the opinion that some part of it is unfit for general exhibition.

The July 1971 List

- Censorship of movies in Dublin first-run cinemas in July 1971: *Dirty Dingus Magee* (general, no cuts), *The Extraordinary Seaman* (general, no cuts), *The Rise and Rise of Michael Rimmer* (Over 16, small cut), *10 Rillington Place* (Over 18, no cuts), *The Watermelon Man* (Appeals Board, Over 16, small cuts), *Getting Straight* (Over 18, no cuts), *The Virgin and the Gypsy* (Appeals Board, Over 16, cuts), *Sabata* (general, no cuts), *Wuthering Heights* (Over 18, no cuts), *Zeppelin* (general, no cuts), *Start the Revolution Without Me* (general, no cuts), *Suppose They Gave a War And Nobody Came* (general no cuts), *The Cheyenne Social Club* (Over 16, no cuts), *Brides of Blood* (Over 12, no cuts), *Little Big Man* (Appeals Board, Over 12, small cut).

- Under Appeal: *Sunday Bloody Sunday, Percy, There's A Girl In My Soup, Villain, Take A Nice Girl Like You, All The Right Noises, Queimada, The Owl And the Pussycat, Five Easy Pieces, BS I Love You, The Statue, Pussycat Pussycat I Love You*

- Banned: *Dorian Grey*

Poor John Schlesinger has again fallen foul to this ludicrously flawed system. Having been forced by distributors to agree to Appeals Board cuts in *Midnight Cowboy*, he now finds that *Sunday Bloody Sunday* has been denied an Irish release by the Film Censor. The decision is being appealed, of course, but even if the banning is overturned, it will probably be on the basis of an Over 18 cert with cuts.

14 August 1971

Father James W Kelly of Headford, Co Galway, in a long letter to the editor, comes up with an insidious justification for the censorship of art. "The art or quality film is much more dangerous than the cheap sex-violence stuff because it is by its very poetry more persuasive. The sex-violence genre is deplorable but by and large, its very crudity defeats ready identification by the viewers: this stuff seems ubiquitous and I would imagine that any censor having to wade through hours of this, the detritus of the permissive age, might well be pardoned if some of the less garish got through. But the public authority has the duty to challenge any public exhibiting of evil, even against the outraged protests of its being art."

29 August 1971

Father Kelly's argument ("art is not autonomous and art for art's sake breaks down when by intent and effect it is seductive towards evil: God's law alone is supreme") emboldens Mr K Whelan from Templeogue to write to the editor demanding my dismissal. "If you accept Fr Kelly's statement — and as a Christian newspaper how can you refute it? — then you must not allow Mr Carty to use your paper as an outlet for his insidious form of pornographic propaganda that is cloaked by shallow intellectualism."

Father Kelly had singled out for attack actresses in French cinema who were on a self-confessed abortion list: "Women responsible in large part for French films have human blood on their hands and have openly flaunted it. Following that, and in general, we need not be too abject in apology to anyone for scrutinising their wares." He also maintained that Jiri Menzel's banned *Closely Observed Trains* while a classic "is also an obscene film in conception with long moments organic to it of palpable sensuality and eroticism... I was ashamed to be there and when I left I felt dirty."

This intolerance proved too much for playwright Hugh Leonard. Father Kelly's misrepresentation of what I was trying to achieve by publishing details of censorship decisions was bad enough. But what appalled Leonard was the "near-sleveenish attack upon the private lives of certain actresses, using this as a kind of justification for not needing to be over-scrupulous about roughing up their films...When he drags private sins into a discussion of censorship, my own reaction is to feel as dirty as he felt after seeing *Closely Observed Trains*.

"What is at issue is not censorship itself, but the incompetence of our censors who on the evidence, have no sympathy with, or understanding of, the works which they outlaw and mutilate...Films which were banned outright here several years ago are now being released uncut. It would be fatuous to ask whether what was immoral and indecent then is no longer so. The truth is, perhaps, that their showing on television has given our censors a shield behind which they can be belatedly courageous. Perhaps in another ten years we will be permitted to see *Closely Observed Trains* and an unsavaged version of *Midnight Cowboy*."

5 September 1971

Sorry, Mr Whelan, I'm still here. Really, I'm not worth your venom. Would it not be more sensible to demolish my arguments or dispute my facts rather than denigrate my character? But then you're merely following the example of Father Kelly who maintains that the worth of a movie is determined by the morality of its makers. A movie involving Romy Schneider or some other actress who advocates changes in the abortion laws of her country is automatically unfit to be seen in Ireland. It is difficult to see where the line might be drawn with such an arbitrary guideline for movies. Is the work of divorced directors to be banned? What if the cameraman is having an affair? Or if one of the actors is an atheist? Ban the movie?

Since we're dealing with the absurd, the Appeals Board has overturned Dr Macken's banning of Bob Rafelson's *Five Easy Pieces*. It's been passed with an Over 18 certificate and one verbal cut — the exclamation Jesus Christ!

18 September 1971

Hugh Leonard and I meet for the first time, discussing film censorship on Gay Byrne's 'Late Late Show'. Leonard is the only prominent figure in the arts so far to come out in public in support of the campaign. Perhaps this reticence reflects the fact that cinema has never been on the right side of the cultural tracks in Ireland. Or maybe it's just the usual Irish practice of playing safe.

The August 1971 List

- Censorship of films in Dublin first-run cinemas in August 1971: *Five Easy Pieces* (Appeals Board, Over 18, one dialogue cut), *A Taste of Honey* (Appeals Board,Over 18, not cuts). *Ja Ja Mein General* (general, no cuts), *Countess Dracula* (Over 18, small cuts), *Things of Life* (Over 18, no cuts), *Back From the Planet Of the Apes* (general, no cuts), *Big Jake* (general, no cuts), *Leo the Last* (Appeals Board, Over 18, cuts), *Flight of the Doves* (general, no cuts), *The Leather Boys* (Appeals Board, resubmitted, Over 18, cuts), *The Bootleggers* (Over 16, cuts)

- Under Appeal: *Summer of 42, Get Carter, The Owl and the Pussycat, Take A Nice Girl Like You, All the Right Noises, Percy, The Statue, The Villain, Sunday Bloody Sunday, Quiemada, Pussycat Pussycat I Love You*

It's been left to ordinary moviegoers to object to the way movies are so routinely mutilated. Which, it turns out, is how Leonard sees himself. He was weaned on westerns and on serials like *King of the Royal Mounted* and *The Clutching Hand* which played at the Picture House, the local cinema in Dun Laoghaire favoured by his foster mother — he never knew his real parents.

"She wouldn't go to the Pavilion because she didn't like to walk up the Marine Road in the wind," he tells me. "I'd get off from the local national school at 3 o'clock, take the tram to Dun Laoghaire, get out at the Picture House, go inside and she'd be there in the front row of the middle stalls, and she'd have a packet of sandwiches and a Baby Power with milk — me lunch."

Leonard has reimagined himself in his plays through the movie forms and themes that captured his imagination back then. Like *King's Row*, the Sam Wood melodrama about young people coming of age, which he saw when he was seventeen. "You identified like mad. You said this could be my small town. The nice thing about *King's Row* is that the town is never seen. So you were able to invent your own town in your head."

Leonard plays have featured in Dublin Theatre Festival most years since his debut with *The Big Birthday* in 1958. He joined Granada television soon after, scripting original plays, adaptations and the farcical series 'Me Mammy'. He wrote the Oscar Werner movie *Interlude*, and also *The Great Catherine* — "a disaster" — for Peter O'Toole.

Percy, a penis transplant comedy starring Elke Sommer, Britt Ekland and Hywel Bennett, which he scripted for Ralph Thomas, has been with the Appeals Board for several weeks. He doesn't expect it to get through, even with cuts. The plot concerns the widow of the donor of a penis who, after several affairs, ends up in bed with the man who received the penis and exclaims: "Welcome home, Percy." The movie has no pretensions to being anything more than rude fun. But why should there be anything wrong with that?

Leonard returned to Ireland in 1970, taking advantage of Charles Haughey's new tax exemption scheme for writers and artists. His television adaptation of his play *Stephen D* is getting its first screening on BBC 2 the following night. He invites us to watch it with him.

Several of the cast — Milo O'Shea, David Kelly, Maureen Toal — are at the small party in his bungalow on Killiney Hill that overlooks the village of Dalkey where he grew up. Noel Pearson, a showband manager who is now becoming something of a theatre impressario, is in expansive form. He seems to have a gambler's instinct for what will work with the public. It wouldn't be a surprise to see him producing movies if the film industry ever gets off the ground. He even has a script ready, based on the life of Brendan Behan.

3 October 1971

Mike Lawler of Guinness Film Society has taken up my plea for a Dublin showing of Andy Warhol's movies. The Society's 1971/72 programme includes Warhol's *Lonesome Cowboys*, along with the banned Philip Roth adaptation *Goodbye Columbus*, Jane Fonda's *Barabella*, Alain Robbe-Grillet's *Trans-Europ Express* and *The Wild Angels*. The proliferation of film societies throughout the country — with Michael Dwyer's in Tralee and George Keegan's in Carrickmacross particularly adventurous — is showing up the hypocritical absurdity of Irish censorship. The same movies that take months to be rejected or cut are available in their original unexpurgated form to club audiences. Like the Contraception Pill, such movies are prohibited but readily available.

Rosemary's Baby proved so popular with students at UCD the other night that a second screening is being arranged. Why is it all right for a member of a film society to see it whereas it would be a perversion of public morality for the same person to see it in a Dublin cinema? Is there a moral difference between a person who is a member of a film society and one who is not? Why is one deemed to be corruptible and the other not? Could it be that club audiences are invariably middle class and therefore in the eyes of the state somehow more to be trusted?

Meanwhile Nik Roeg and Donald Cammell's *Performance*, which has already been screened by film societies, has been belatedly passed by the Appeals Board: over 18 and cuts, of course. Similarly with John Cassavetes' *Husbands*.

31 October 1971

By my count, at least twenty-one movies are now held up at the Appeals Board. There's a danger that distributors may not even try for a Irish release with some of their more challenging movies. The Censor won't get a chance to ban Ken Russell's *The Devils*, which deals with the apparent demonic possession of a convent of nuns in seventeenth-century France: Warners have no plans to submit it to him.

Two pages of cuts — about one and a half minutes — recommended by the British Board of Film Control had been agreed to by Russell before it was released with an X certificate in the UK. Even then there was an outcry from the new National

---

The September 1971 List

- Censorship of movies screened in September 1971: *Performance* (Appeals Board, Over 18, cuts), *The Travelling Executioner* (Appeals Board, Over 16, cuts), *House of the Dark Shadows* (general, no cuts), *Lawman* (Over 16, cuts), *Cotton Comes to Harlem* (Over 18, cuts), *Murphy's War* (over 16, cuts), *Husbands* (Appeals Board, Over 18, cuts). *The Sweet Sins of Sexy Susan* (Over 18, cuts), *The McMasters* (Over 16, no cuts), *Le Grand Amour* (general, no cuts), *The Great White Hope* (Over 16, no cuts), *Carry On Henry* (Over 16, cuts)

- Under Appeal: *The Hunting Party, Country Dance, Vanishing Point, A Severed Head, Investigation of a Citizen Above Suspicion, Serafino, Queimada, BS I Love You, Take a Nice Girl Like You, Sunday Bloody Sunday, Summer of 42, Percy, Get Carter, A Day In the Life Of Ivan Denisovitch, Villain*

Festival of Light led by Mary Whitehouse and Lord Longford's Committee on Pornography. With the surprise election of a Tory Government and growing political unrest following the passing of the repressive Industrial Relations Act and the introduction of internment in Northern Ireland, Britain seems to be experiencing something of a right-wing puritan backlash. It's not likely to help the case against censorship here.

Whatever about distributors not bothering to submit movies that might be troublesome, the good news is that the producers of John Schlesinger's *Sunday Bloody Sunday* are so far refusing to permit it to be shown in the mutilated form proposed by the Appeals Board (who are only prepared to pass it on condition several sequences are cut, including the celebrated homosexual kiss between Peter Finch and Murray Head).

Meanwhile Mr Dennis Coakley, the assistant secretary at the Department of Justice who banned *Closely Observed Trains* when he deputised for the Censor last year, has been in action

---

The October 1971 List

- Censorship of movies screened in October 1971: *Vanishing Point* (Appeals Board, Over 16, small cuts), *The Statue* (Appeals Board, Over 18 cuts), *Love With A Proper Stranger* (Appeals Board, resubmitted, Over 18, no cuts), *Cold Turkey* (general, no cuts), *There's A Girl In My Soup* (Appeals Board, Over 18, cuts), *You Can't Have Everything* (Over 16, cuts), *Connecting Rooms* (Over 18, cuts), *Darker Than Amber* (Over 16, no cuts), *Joaquin Murieta* (general, cuts), *The Soldier Who Declared Peace* (general, no cuts), *I Walk the Line* (Over 16, no cuts), *I Never Sang For My Father* (general, cuts), *The Ballad of Cable Hogue* (Over 16, no cuts), *The Wild Country* (general, no cuts), *Quest for Love* (Over 16, no cuts)

- Under Appeal: *Bloody Mama, Making It, A Quiet Day in the Country, Doctors' Wives, Sunday Bloody Sunday, Take A Nice Girl Like You, Summer of 42, Tom Jones, The Hunting Party, A Severed Head, Chastity, Up Pompeii, BS I Love you, Percy, Villain, Get Carter, Country Dance, A Day In The Life of Ivan Denisovitch, Pussycat Pussycat I Love You, Serafino, The Touch*

again. He made a small cut in the Alistair MacLean spy thriller, *Puppet On A Chain*.

5 December 1971

John Schlesinger is still withholding his consent to cuts demanded by the Appeals Board in *Sunday Bloody Sunday*. He has been joined by Robert Mulligan, who is refusing to allow cuts in *Summer of 42*.

Maybe it will be possible in the coming year to rally international directors to the campaign against censorship in Ireland by alerting them to what is happening to their movies and encouraging them to refuse to collaborate. The difficulty is that often they have little power once they have handed over their movies to distributors. What would happen if Ingmar Bergman,

---

The November 1971 List

- Censorship of movies screened in November 1971: *The Subject Was Roses* (Over 18, cuts), *Quiemada* (Appeals Board, Over 16, no cuts), *Investigation of a Citizen Above Suspicion* (Appeals Board, Over 18, cuts), *Medium Cool* (Over 18, cuts), *Valdez Is Coming* (Appeals Board, Over 18, cuts), *Carry On Up the Jungle* (Appeals Board, Over 16, cuts), *Jenny* (Over 18, no cuts), *A Town Called Bastard* (Appeals Board, Over 18, cuts), *Figures In a Landscape* (Over 18, no cuts), *Girl in a Car with Glasses and a Gun* (Over 16, cuts), *Jane Eyre* (Over 16, no cuts), *Hands of the Ripper* (Over 18, no cuts), *Violent City* (Appeals Board, Over 16, cuts), *Puppet on a Chain* (general, cut), *SWALK* (Under 12, no cuts), *The Grissom Gang* (Over 18, no cuts), *Willard* (general, no cuts), *The Samourai* (general, no cuts), *Zachariah* (general, no cuts), *The Last Valley* (Over 18, cuts), *My Sweet Charles* (Over 18, no cuts)

- Under Appeal: *Loot, Puzzle of a Downfall Child, Little Murders, Making It, Revenge, A Severed Head, Serafino, The Seven Minutes, The Hunting Party, MOVE, Pussycat Pussycat I Love You, One Brief Summer, Take A Nice Girl Like You, Chastity, Up Pompeii, BS I Love You, Doctors' Wives, Marriage of a Young Stockbroker, Country Dance, The Touch, A Day In the Life of Ivan Denisovich, Pursuit in Needle Park, Bloody Mama, Percy*

whose latest movie *The Touch* has just been banned — the Censor is nothing if not consistent in his treatment of the great Swedish director — refused to allow his movies to be shown in Ireland? Or Fellini? Or Antonioni?

Two movies which were savagely mutilated by the Censor several years ago have now been passed without cuts by the Appeals Board. They are Tony Richardson's *Tom Jones*, screened originally in Dublin in 1964 with twenty-one cuts, and Joseph Losey's *The Servant*, scripted by Harold Pinter, which was shorn of virtually any suggestion of homosexual attraction between Dirk Bogarde and his valet, James Fox.

Such a divergence in standards in such a short time suggests that the censorship authorities who presume to be our moral guardians are uncertain about what is or is not indecent or obscene. How can it be that *The Servant* would have corrupted me in 1964 but is no longer a threat to my moral welfare in 1971?

9 January 1972

The monthly censorship black-list has completed its first year. Of the 255 movies listed, 103 went to the Appeals Board, 22 were banned, 43 were passed on appeal, 26 are still awaiting decision on appeal, and 12 await release. Of the 195 movies screened, 73 were cut and of these 45 were Over 18 and 22 Over 16. Of the 43 movies passed on appeal, 35 were cut: 27 of these were over 18 and 7 were over 16.

It is clear from the titles of movies submitted that hardcore pornography of the kind causing so much concern in the US is not a problem here. Dublin audiences got no nearer than the risible *Beyond the Valley of the Dolls* and *Myra Breckinridge* — both banned on appeal — to anything approaching a 'sexploitation' movie.

It is clear that the Appeals Board has now become an alternative censorship board rather than the final arbitrer in exceptional cases. Forty percent of the movies on our lists were taken to the Appeals Board. This suggests that the standards applied by the Censor are out of sympathy with contemporary cinema. The purely voluntary Appeals Board is becoming swamped by the amount of work it must handle: by the end of 1971 at least 26 movies were still awaiting decisions.

It is clear that Irish film censorship is obssessively concerned with protecting the morals of adults. Nearly half the movies restricted to adults were cut. The more adult the audience, the more likely cuts became. 53.6 percent of over 18 movies were cut, 41.5 percent of over 16, 14.3 percent of under 12 with adult and 9.6 percent of general audience movies.

It is clear that the more important and acclaimed a director, the more likely it is that his movies will be cut or banned.

It is clear that the Appeals Board rivals the Censor in its ruthlessness. Cuts were made in eighty-one percent of movies passed on appeal, despite the fact that all but two of them carried Over 18 or Over 16 certificates. The chairman of the Appeals

---

The December 1971 List

- Censorship of movies screened in December 1971: *Nicholas and Alexandra* (Under 12, no cuts), *Five Easy Pieces* (Appeals Board, Over 16, cuts), *Traffic* (general, no cuts), *Creatures The World Forgot* (Over 16, no cuts), *For Singles Only* (Over 16, cuts), *The Gallery Murders* (Over 18, cuts), *The French Connection* (Over 16, no cuts), *Le Mans* (general, no cuts), *Fiddler on the Roof* (general, no cuts), *One More Train to Rob* (general, no cuts), *Raid on Rommel* (general, no cuts), *Please, Sir* (general, no cuts), *Fools* (Over 18, cuts), *Change of Mind* (Over 16, cuts), *Sweden Heaven and Hell* (Over 18, cuts), *Uptight* (Over 18, no cuts), *Punchup in Istanbul* (Over 18, no cuts), *Hells Angels on Wheels* (Over 18, no cuts), *All the Way Up* (Over 18, no cuts), *The Engagement* (general, cuts), *Conquista* (general, no cuts), *Mark of the Tiger* (general, no cuts)
- Under Appeal: *Outback, Koch, A Quiet Place in the Country, Bananas, The Ballad of Tam Lin, Doughters of Darkness, The Hunting Party, BS I Love You, Little Murders, One Brief Summer, Chastity, Bloody Mamma, Percy, Marriage of a Young Stockbroker, MOVE, The Seven Minutes, Panic in Needle Park, Loot, A Severed Head, Doctors' Wives, Serafino, Take A Nice Girl Like You, Puzzle of a Downfall Child, The Hired Hand*
- Banned: *Up Pompeii*

Board is Judge Conor Maguire, the current members are John JF Carroll, Rev John Desmond Nurray, John O'Connor, District Justice Alfred Rochford, Mrs Helena Ruttledge, Dermot Breen, Mrs Isabelle Byrne, Father Richard O'Donoghue.

Whether publication of the monthly list of censorship decisions will force any change in the system is still problematical, although response from moviegoers has been encouraging. But at least it enables the public to form their own judgement about the working of a censorship system that insists on making all its decisions in secret.

Whatever the outcome, technology is soon likely to make the entire issue of cinema censorship redundant. Satellite tie-ups will enable people to tune into film channels anywhere in the world. A sign of the times is tonight's screening on BBC of John Schlesinger's *Darling*, which is still banned in Ireland. What does the Government intend to do to prevent us watching this movie that is supposedly subversive of public morality? Seize all of the TV sets?

24 January 1972

I receive the annual Showcase Award for Significant Contribution to Cinema in 1971, at a dinner in Jury's Hotel. The award is handed over to me by Harry Band. I remark, with an accuracy that is perhaps not fully appreciated by many of those present, that I could not continue doing what I am doing without the support of Harry and other people in the industry.

6 February 1992

Even by Roman Catholic standards, Irish movie censorship appears to be unduly cautious and conservative. There are significant deviations between the ratings published by the National Catholic Office of Motion Pictures in America and the decisions reached here during the past year by the Censor and the Appeals Board.

Several movies labelled "unobjectionable for adults with reservations" were banned in Ireland. These include *Boys In the Band, Goodbye Columbus, Hard Contract* and *Last Summer.* Other movies listed in this category that were severely cut by the Irish Censor or Appeals Board were *The Damned, Satyricon, Midnight Cowboy* and *Secret Ceremony.*

In *The Word*, a magazine published by the Divine Word Missionaries in Roscommon, *Sunday Bloody Sunday*, which the Appeals Board wants to cut, has been acclaimed as "a notable piece of cinema". Reviewer Maryvonne Butcher says that while it "does not tell an edifying story, it is so honest, so minutely observed that though like life itself, it may be shocking, it teaches one a great deal about compassion, tolerance and the faculty of loving."

Yet the Appeals Board sees it as a menace in its original form, demanding so many cuts that director John Schlesinger has so far refused his consent.

The January 1972 List

- Censorship of movies screened in January 1972: *The Owl And the Pussycat* (Appeals Board, Over 18, 90 feet cut), *Diamonds Are Forever* (general, 58 feet cut), *Diary of a Mad Housewife* (Over 18, cuts), *Zita* (Over 16, cuts), *Shootout* (Under 12, with adult, no cuts), *Code Name Kill* (general, no cuts), *Shaft* (Over 18, cuts), *A Day in the Life of Ivan Denisovich* (Appeals Board, general, no cuts), *On the Buses* (Over 18, cuts), *Pigsty* (Appeals Board, Over 18, 180 feet cut)

- Under Appeal: *Doctors' Wives, Loot, The Hired Hand, Bloody Mamma, Chastity, Percy, BS I Love You, Brief Summer, MOVE, Marriage of a Young Stockbroker, Little Murders, Daughters of Darkness, The Ballad of Tam Lin, Koch, The Straw Dogs, The Touch, A Quiet Place in the Country, The Hunting Party, Pussycat Pussycat I Love You, Where's Poppa, Burke and Hare*

- Banned: *Take A Girl Like You, Making It, Panic In Needle Park*

15 February 1972

I take part with Hugh Leonard in a debate on censorship at Dun Laoghaire Junior Chamber of Commerce. I send off letters to Antonioni, Schlesinger, Fellini and Bergman, drawing their attention to the situation in Irish censorship and asking for their comments.

3 March 1972

About 100 people walk out of the Rupert Guinness Hall during a screening of Andy Warhol's *Lonesome Cowboys*. Others stay and applaud. The polarised reaction is not surprising. Last year police raided a London club during a screening of Warhol's *Flesh*. In 1968 the premiere of another Warhol movie was busted by New York police. Yet many eminent and respectable critics, notably Dilys Powell, have expressed respect and admiration for Warhol's approach to cinema. If they are right — and I believe they are — tonight's screening will be something of a landmark in cinema in Ireland.

In outline *Lonesome Cowboys* might seem pornographic and blasphemous. A man and women strip each other and appear to copulate. Homosexuals flirt and sleep together. There are images showing men in drag, cunnilingus, various types of fetishism and a seduction performed to the chant of Kyrie Eleison. Yet the effect is totally unerotic and unsensational. Warhol's intention is not to create an illusion of reality or a titillating spectacle but to observe actuality. Unlike conventional Hollywood 'pretend' movies, which exploit sex by setting up erotic situations which purport to represent real life, Warhol movies simply confront behaviour as it is. In *Lonesome Cowboys* the western formula is used to provide a framework within which the Warhol factory team of Viva, Tom Hompertz, Joe D'Allesandro, Louis Waldon, Francis Francine and Taylor Mead re-enact their relationships and inner feelings and impulses. It is an unscripted record of how they are prepared to behave before the camera.

Like Godard, Warhol keeps emphasising the presence of the camera. He flicks the switch on and off, causing quick jumps in sound and picture. Heads are decapitated by the frame. Wind blurs the soundtrack. Damaged and overexposed film is projected. Figures move in and out of focus unintentionally. The emphasis is on everything that happens rather than on takes selected to suggest a prestyled reality. No attempt is made to conceal the artificiality of the painted Arizona backdrop. Unrelated figures, possibly visitors to the set, can be glimpsed momentarily in some of the takes.

The people in the movie were given a brief outline of the setup and allowed take the action from there themselves. They were not so much improvising as being themselves. The camera simply runs and records everything indiscriminately. The effect is frequently broad humour, the incongruity of the sham western setting counterpointing the contemporary dialogue and attitudes. It's at times tedious, embarrassing, shocking, and funny. It is Warhol's vision of his own world and the people and ideas that inform it.

5 March 1972

The official Censor is unwell. Political approaches have been made to Conor O'Brien — by now I am his deputy editor — suggesting that we call off the campaign out of consideration for Dr Macken's condition. It is a worrying suggestion, but there can be only one response. Since before Christmas many of the movies submitted for censorship have been viewed by Ms S Ni Thuathaigh, a higher executive officer at the Department of Justice. The immediate effect has been a significant drop in the number of movies going before the Appeals Board.

Ms Ni Thuathaigh appears to be rejecting fewer movies and, with certain exceptions, demanding fewer cuts. This should give the Appeals Board time to clear some of the large backlog of movies awaiting decision, among them Bergman's *The Touch*, Elio Petri's *A Quiet Place In The Country*, Stuart Rosenberg's

MOVE and Carl Reiner's *Where's Poppa*. Sadly in its eagerness to clear the deck, it has banned Roger Corman's *Marriage of a Young Stockbroker* and Hugh Leonard's penis transplant comedy *Percy*. *Chastity*, which had been awaiting a decision for several months, has been withdrawn by its distributors because their rights to it had expired.

7 March 1972

Two special branch detectives visit me at the office. They want me to make a statement that I am the writer of the report on the screening of *Lonesome Cowboys* that appeared in the *Sunday Independent*. The Gardai have received complaints about the screening and need my statement in order to prepare a prosecution against Mike Lawler and Guinness Film Society. I refuse to make a statement.

The February 1972 List

- Censorship of movies screened in February 1972: *Blue Water, White Death* (general, no cuts), *Family Life* (Appeals Board, Over 16, four-letter words cut), *Waltz of the Torreadors* (Appeals Board, Over 16, no cuts), *The Deserter and the Nomads* (Appeals Board, Over 18, no cuts), *A Severed Head* (Appeals Board, Over 16, cuts), *Doc* (Over 16, 60 feet cut), *The Red Baron* (general, no cuts), *Bed And Board* (Over 16, no cuts), *99 Women* (Over 18, cuts), *A Gunfight* (general, no cuts), *Squeeze a Flower* (general, no cuts), *The Jigsaw Murder* (Over 16, no cuts), *Twins of Evil* (Over 18, no cuts), *Twiggy* (general, no cuts), *Hells Belles* (Over 18, no cuts), *The Moonshine War* (Over 18, cuts), *The Adding Machine* (Over 16, no cuts), *Revenge* (Appeals Board, Over 18, 90 feet cut), *The Rage Within* (Over 18, cuts)
- Under Appeal: *Pretty Maids All In A Row, Backstreet, School for Virgins, The Touch, One Brief Summer, A Quiet Place in the Country, Outback, MOVE, Daughters of Darkness, The Ballad of Tam Lin, BS I Love You, The Hunting Party, Pussycat Pussycat I Love You, Loot, Doctors' Wives, Little Murders, Where's Poppa? Burke and Hare, The Straw Dogs*
- Banned: *Marriage of a Young Stockbroker, Percy, Bloody Mamma*
- Withdrawn: *Chastity*

The editor has received a pile of letters attacking me not just for reviewing *Lonesome Cowboys* but for reviewing it so favourably. Father Brian Magee of Blackrock believes that I have a good cause but that I am "destroying it through overstating it. This latest outburst leaves him isolated from the vast majority of reasonable people who are sincerely worried about the future of our society, people whose Christian principles prevent them from accepting just anything in the name of art." Ms Mary Brogan of Fairview is "absolutely appalled... Surely the whole subject matter is wrong and sinful and against the whole concept of the dignity of mankind?" Mr J Murphy suggests that I suffer "from an intellectual inferiority complex. His bandwagoning with the heavy intellectuals is simply a defence mechanism against a feeling of personal inadequacy. This could explain his constant attribution of high art to the peepshow type of film currently favoured by the intellectuals."

9 March 1972

As I arrive home from work, I notice the two Special Branch men talking with a neighbour. I wave to them. They try to look invisible.

12 March 1972

A response from Michaelango Antonioni. "In reference to your letter, I am not astonished, I am deeply angered. To cut a film made with artistical intent is an insult not only to the author but to the culture and the public.

"I don't know what kind of cuts they made to my film — *Zabriskie Point* — but in any case they do reveal lack of sensitivity and narrow-minded moralism.

"You may publish these statements because I would like everyone to know exactly what I think of censorship.

"I greatly appreciate your informing me of this situation in Ireland. This support consoles me, in a way, for the bitterness of the news you have sent me."

19 March 1972

John Schlesinger was briefly in Dublin but unable to contact me. He leaves me a letter instead. "I do feel strongly about censorship and believe that there is no justification for it. John Trevelyan (secretary of the British Board of Film Control) once said to me that if he allowed me to make *A Kind of Loving* and include scenes which dealt with contraception that it would open the flood gates for people to copy. When he finally saw the film he agreed that we had presented it in such a way that no offence was caused and everything was allowed to stay as it was. I do not think that you can penalise serious film makers because of the numerous mountebanks that adorn our profession and I believe that you must trust artists to be their own censors and endeavour to play up and not down to audiences' intelligence.

"In Ireland it seems ridiculous that an outmoded method of censorship can prevent films from being shown, when the very things they wish to have censored are freely available on television. I resist cuts that make my films meaningless and, therefore, for a long time would not allow *Midnight Cowboy* to be shown, and only did so finally after great pressure from the distributors. The cuts suggested for *Sunday Bloody Sunday* are so extreme as to render the film meaningless, and I would prefer to withhold it from Ireland until such time as somebody comes to their senses. Finally, unfortunately, the distributors can always override my decisions and may show the film without my consent, which they are quite free to do if I am not personally prepared to make the cuts."

8 April 1972

I sit by my father's bed in the Mater Nursing Home and watch him die. My mother holds his hand. On the table by his bed are Richard Ellmann's *Selected Essays* and a book of David Frost interviews, with notes for a review he was writing. Tom Reilly had finally persuaded him to stop smoking when he was fifty-nine. Almost his last words are: "I don't know whether it was worth it."

Later an aide guides a blind eighty-nine-year-old Eamonn de Valera to the bed where he is laid out. De Valera touches his hand. The room is silent. A police motorcycle escort clears the way through rush hour traffic to Star of the Sea Church in Sandymount. The last time I was there was for our wedding. I saw tears in my father's eye. He always cried when he was happy.

10 April 1972

Federico Fellini joins in the attack on Irish censorship in the form of a reply to my letter about the cuts made in *Satyricon*. His reply (in French) is written on his behalf by Gerald Morin, for some

---

The March 1972 List

- Censorship of movies screened in March 1972: *Klute* (Over 18, small cuts), *Wild Rovers* (general, no cuts), *A Bullet for Pretty Boy* (Over 18, no cuts), *Green Slime* (Over 18, no cuts), *The Anderson Tapes* (Appeals Board, Over 18, words 'Jesus Christ' cut), *Catch A Spy for Me* (general, no cuts), *Find A Place to Die* (Over 12, no cuts), *Galleon of the Slaves* (Over 12, cuts), *On A Clear Day You Can See Forever* (general no cuts), *I Killed Rasputin* (Over 12, no cuts) *Captain Apache* (Over 18, cuts), *The Abominable Dr Phibes* (Over 16, no cuts)
- Under Appeal: *Pretty Maids All in a Row, BS I Love You, One Brief Summer, MOVE, Little Murders, Doctors' Wives, Seven Minutes, Pussycat Pussycat I Love You, Burke and Hare, The Touch, The Straw Dogs, Ballad of Tam Lin, School For Virgins*
- Banned: *Loot*

years his secretary and assistant director. "Monsieur Fellini wishes me to tell you that he is opposed to all censorship which reduces the audience to the mortifying position of a grotesque and unreal infantilism. Censorship is never a solution, it is only a palliative. It resolves nothing. It is like a prison that tries to suppress a problem without treating it.

"Every society has its censors, but who educates these censors? Their decisions are often determined by the appropriateness of a work at a particular time, but on what is their criterion of appropriateness based?

"Rather than censor the author, it is better to educate the public."

7 May 1972

The monthly clandestine list of censorship statistics indicates a significant decrease in the number of movies being cut or rejected by the Censor and the Appeals Board.

Several movies sent for appeal, such as Alan Pakula's conspiracy thriller *Klute* and Milos Forman's American drug satire *Taking Off*, have been passed either with minor cuts or no cuts at all.

There are hopeful signs that the authorities may finally be accepting the argument that movies should be evaluated in terms

---

The April 1972 List

- Censorship of movies screened in April 1972: *A Quiet Day in the Country* (Appeals Board, Over 18, small cut), *The Hunting Game* (Appeals Board, Over 18, no cuts), *Where's Poppa?* (Appeals Board, Over 18, cut), *Play Misty For Me* (Appeals Board, Over 18, cut), *Run Angel Run* (Over 18, no cuts), *Strip Poker* (Over 18, no cuts), *Charro* (general, no cuts), *The Only Way Out Is Dead* (general, no cuts)
- Under Appeal: *Burke And Hare, One Brief Summer, MOVE, Little Murders, Seven Minutes, Daughters of Darkness, The Straw Dogs*
- Banned: *Pretty Maids All in a Row*

of their overall merit as art. The frame-by-frame moralistic approach, which led to the mutilation of *Secret Ceremony, The Damned, Midnight Cowboy* and *Zabriskie Point*, no longer seems to be in favour.

"There's a great deal of rethinking going on," one of my sources, Harry Band, informs me. Another source, Gerry Duffy, says: "If it keeps on like this, the Appeals Board will be complaining because they'll have nothing to do."

The more broadminded approach coincides with a period during which two higher executive officers from the Department of Justice Ms S Ni Thuathaigh and Mr P McMahon have in effect taken over the duties of the Censor, Dr Christopher Macken, who is seriously ill. It suggests that the Government may finally have come to recognise that film censorship is too repressive. Could this be the start of a process of *de facto* liberalisation?

11 June 1972

It's still too soon to celebrate, but a radical change seems to have occurred in the Government's approach to film censorship. As always it is being carried out behind closed doors, without debate or discussion, but its effect is clearly evident in the monthly unofficial censorship lists compiled by the *Sunday Independent*. These reveal that no cut has been made in any movie of importance during the past few weeks (apart from a slight snip in Bob Fosse's *Cabaret*).

Robert Altman's *Images* and Paul Medak's *The Ruling Class*, both shown at Cannes Film Festival, have been passed without cuts. So have Arthur Hiller's medical satire *Hospital*, Paul Newman's *Never Give An Inch*, Roman Polanski's *Macbeth*, Don Siegal's *Dirty Harry*, Bo Widerberg's *The Ballad of Joe Hill* and Sidney Pollack's *A Cool Breeze*. Other uncut movies include *A New Leaf, Norwood, Plaza Suite, The Sitting Target, The Carey Treatment* and *The Honkers*. The Appeals Board, which was swamped with a three-month backlog at the end of last year, has virtually run out of movies.

My sources are feeding back to me tantalising details about what is happening at Harcourt Terrace. A triumvirate of civil servants is now effectively in control of censorship in the prolonged absence of Dr Macken. They are Ms Ni Tuathaigh, Mr P McMahon and Mr C Crowley. Together they constitute a *de facto* censorship board somewhat similar to that advocated in our campaign. By not cutting important movies and by allowing this "board" to come into existence, the authorities appear to have tacitly conceded two major demands in the campaign for the overhaul of censorship.

It would be unfair, however, to expect civil servants to carry out censorship on a permanent basis. The Government ought to give *de jure* validity to these changes by amending the Censorship Act and also by appointing censors capable of judging movies on their creative merit. It should be written into the act a) that anybody given power to censor movies must be professionally experienced in cinema; b) that no cuts be made in Over 18 movies; c) that movies be judged on their overall treatment and by the intention of their directors rather than on a frame by frame basis; d) that details of censorship decision be

---

The May 1972 List

- Censorship of movies screened in May 1972: *Je t'aime, Je t'aime* (Over 16, no cuts), *Country Dance* (Appeals Board, Over 18, small cut), *The Andromeda Strain* (Over 12, no cuts), *Red Sky in the Morning* (Over 16, no cuts), *Cat o' Nine Tails* (Over 16, small cut), *The Satanists* (Over 16, no cuts), *Blood On Satan's Claw* (Over 16, no cuts), *Doctors' Wives* (Appeals Board, Over 18, cuts), *Pussycat Pussycat I Love You* (Appeals Board, Over 16, no cuts), *Outback* (Appeals Board, Over 16, small cuts), *Carry On At Your Convenience* (Over 16, no cuts), *The Beguiled* (Appeals Board, Over 18, small cuts), *The Challengers* (general, no cuts), *Companeros* (Over 16, no cuts), *Commandos* (Over 16, no cuts), *One of Those Things* (Appeals Board, Over 18, cuts), *Explosion* (Appeals Board, Over 18, cuts), *Love of Life* (general, no cuts), *Beast in the Cellar* (Over 16, no cuts), *Time For Loving* (Over 18, small cut)
- Under Appeal: *The Straw Dogs, Daughters of Darkness, MOVE, Little Murders, One Brief Summer*

published regularly and the censor be required to answer to the public for his/her decisions.

21 June 1972

Dr Macken has died after an illness of several months. His successor as Censor is Dermot Breen, who has been a member of the Appeals Board for the last three years. He founded the Cork International Film Festival — Ireland's first — in 1955 and has been its director ever since. During that time he used the Festival to introduce Irish audiences to the work of many leading directors, with particular emphasis on short films. I ring up to wish him well and he agrees to a wide-ranging interview as soon as he has settled in. It will be the first interview given by a Film Censor about his work and heralds a new openness in the operation of film censorship.

The June 1972 List

- Censorship of movies screened in June 1972: *No Blade of Grass* (Over 18, cuts), *The Last Run* (Over 18, cuts), *Images* (Over 18, no cuts), *Soul to Soul* (general, no cuts), *The Red Tent* (general, no cuts), *Unman, Wittering and Zigo* (Over 18, cuts), *The Hospital* (Over 18, no cuts), *The Honkers* (Over 16, no cuts), *The Crook* (general, no cuts), *Zee & Co* (Over 18, no cuts), *Murders in Rue Morgue* (Over 18, no cuts), *Return of Count Yorga* (Over 18, no cuts), *The Deserter* (Over 12, no cuts), *Cisco Pike* (Over 18, no cuts), *Little Fauss and Big Halsy* (Over 12, cuts), *Friends* (Appeals Board, Over 18, cuts), *Let's Scare Jessica To Death* (Over 16, cuts), *The Ballad of Joe Hill* (Over 16, slight cut), *Play Misty for Me* (Over 18, no cuts), *Anthony and Cleopatra* (general, no cuts), *Quackser Fortune Has A Cousin In the Bronx* (general, no cuts)
- Under Appeal: *WUSA, Made For Each Other, The Straw Dogs, Such Good Friends, Fine Cut, MOVE, Daughters of Darkness, Little Murders, Angels Who Burn Their Wings, One Brief Summer, The Culpepper Cattle Company, I'll Take Sweden*

16 July 1972

It is too soon yet to say what kind of censor Dermot Breen is going to be. But sadly the Appeals Board is still busy cutting movies by major directors. Ingmar Bergman's *The Touch* has been cut: by now he must be Ireland's most censored director.

It's surprising to find Alfred Hitchcock in difficulties. Ms Ni Thuathaigh, acting as censor, demanded several cuts in his new thriller *Frenzy*. The Appeals Board cancelled some of these, but insisted on removing about sixty feet before granting an Over 18 certificate. Having seen the movie twice at this year's Cannes Festival and interviewed Hitchcock about it, I find the decision baffling. As indeed would Princess Grace, who starred in Hitchcock's to *Catch a Thief* and *Rear Window* in the 1950s, and was in Cannes to lead a standing ovation for *Frenzy*.

Hopefully this will be a temporary aberration before Dermot Breen has a chance to inaugurate a new era in Irish film censorship. The good news is that Francis Ford Coppola's *The Godfather* has been passed without cuts.

24 July 1972

It's a squat, redbrick building beside the police station in Harcourt Terrace, across the road from the home of Micheal MacLiammoir and Hilton Edwards. Dermot Breen unlocks the door to let me in: I get the feeling I'm entering a tomb. "Why not look around first?" He appears cool in a lightweight blue suit, pale blue shirt and blue tie.

He shows me the viewing theatre, a barren auditorium with a cluster of desks facing a wide screen across an empty floor. Off a corridor outside, are locked vaults containing the records of censorship decisions going back to the 1920s. They are still classified as state secrets. Breen tells me that each of his predecessors made annual reports on their work. These are classified as well.

We sit at a long table in the board room. Stacks of trade magazines fill a shelf. Leslie Halliwell's *The Filmgoer's Companion* lies beside the phone.

We break the ice by talking about childhood movies. One of the complaints about Irish censorship has been that it is implemented by people without experience in cinema. Nobody could say that of Breen.

"I've always been interested in cinema, ever since the days of the four-penny hops as a boy. That's why I got involved in amateur theatre and directed many plays. It was the nearest I could get to making films. I even managed a cinema for several years. It's what led me to starting Cork Film Festival."

So what is his taste in movies?

"I've a very catholic taste, catholic with a small 'c'. I like to be entertained basically and I don't like to attend cinema as an exercise. But everyone has their own set of standards.

"I find and I'm sure you probably find too that no matter how bad a film is, if you're interested in cinema there's some good in it and you'll carry something away from it.

"I think it's bad to read about a film in advance. I like to keep my mind objective. Yet even so I find that in the five weeks so far as Censor, there are pictures that I look forward to seeing, that I'd have gone to commercially, and there are others that I think: 'my God, I've got to sit through this!'"

"This is an approach I'll try to maintain, so that I'll never sit and do my job and put myself merely in the position of Censor. If you were to approach the job too clinically, it would become an impossible chore."

I tell him it's encouraging to hear him say this. To often it has seemed as if censors scrutinise everything with a magnifying glass, hardly seeing the movie as a whole but peering at every word and image for harmful implications.

"A lot of people have the idea that the censor is there merely to wield the scissors. The very last thing I want to do is to reach for the scissors. If the Censor has to reach for the scissors, he must do it carefully, with a lot of consideration for the film and for the people who worked so hard to make it and for the audience who are going to see it. He can't just take chunks out indiscriminately.

"There are some words that I am vehemently opposed to. But there was a censorship case recently where if I had taken out this word the whole sentence would have lost meaning and the whole scene would have lost meaning. So I had to weigh the balance, hoping that the public wouldn't pounce on me because I left the word in one instance and took it out in several other instances.

"The same applies to the Holy Name. Now I don't like the Holy Name being used on the stage or screen. But there are times when it is not blasphemous. There are emotional circumstances when the normal reaction of a person would be to utter the Holy Name. It would be more as a prayer than as a rude word. I had a picture the other day where the character used the Holy Name about four times in a scene so effectively and so emotionally that to have taken it out would have been a desecration because it was a prayer, the man was so shocked by the situation. So I left it in."

Twenty years ago most movies were made for a mass audience, but now many are aimed at minority audiences. Should a censor not bear this in mind and treat each movie on the basis of the kind of audience for whom it is intended?

"The Censor is restricted in the way he can control a film. He can give it an age restriction but he's got to assume that a wide conglomerate group of people will see it. He's got to take a broad view. It's all very well to say, as you do, that great directors should be treated as special cases. But it would be bad for a censor to say that because a picture is made by such and such a director, that therefore it can't be wrong."

But if the movie is restricted to Over 18 audiences, surely the audience is adult enough to see for itself and make its own moral judgement or otherwise?

"There must be a limitation on what can be shown on the screen. You know better than I do that it has always been a great danger, indeed it has become common practice to extend sex and violence scenes for purely box-office reasons or because a director enjoys indulging in his fantasies. He tries to shock as much as possible. For instance, I can't understand this idea of keeping the camera on a man being killed while plastic bags of blood burst open. Who wants to look at this sort of thing? It's not entertainment.

"I interpret a film through what I would like my children, and they range in age from ten to nineteen, to see. The kind of book I might like to read I won't leave lying around at home for my son to read. I certainly wouldn't put a picture on the wall that I thought might give my children wrong ideas about life. I'm sure you too as a journalist must draw the line on the type of pictures you reproduce and the language you print."

Well we do draw a line, I tell him, but it is changing all the time. And anyway, newspapers are invariably seen by children. They can't be given an Over 18 certificate.

"But can you guarantee that an Over 18 film will not be seen by children?"

The vast majority aren't. There may be exceptions, as with under-age drinking. But to sanitise every movie on this basis would be absurdly paternalistic. Yet this is what has happened in Ireland. Over 18 movies, particularly by major directors, are cut more frequently and drastically than any others.

"Of course you're looking at it from a different point of view."

Everyone looks at it from a different point of view. Surely that's the whole point. There should be a tolerance of this plurality. "I've seen pictures by top directors and some of the scenes are very unsavoury indeed. I feel that if you were to allow them in, public opinion would very strongly disapprove."

You found them so, and others might find them so, but you could be wrong. Is art to be limited by what current popular opinion regards as morally acceptable? Should a censor take on the function of moral conscience for the adult population?

"But there's always this problem that if one director gets away with it, then all directors can get away with it."

That's not an insurmountable problem. There's no need to treat serious cinema in the same way that you would treat hard-core pornography.

"We have certain moral standards that we must uphold. I'm appointed by the Minister and given a certain job to do. There are certain (I won't say restrictions) but guidelines laid down. I try to follow these as best I can and be as flexible as I can. But there are limitations."

Talking about limitations, if you cut a movie, shouldn't people be informed? It's hardly fair that a person who pays to see the Oscar-winning *Midnight Cowboy* in fact sees an abridged version of it without being told.

"It's not a matter I've had a chance to give any thought to. I don't feel it would serve any useful purpose to advertise whether a film had been cut or not. I think that commercially it wouldn't do any good, it might keep people away."

But why should the public be hoodwinked into paying for something they're not going to get. Whatever about indicating on the certificate if cuts have been made, surely the Censor should be obliged to provide this information to the media. Why the secrecy?

"This is really a matter for the distributors. Give me another month or two. I think that there is an atmosphere now for more communication with the public. After all, it is they who ultimately call the tune."

Distributors have indicated to me that they would have no objection to this information being made available. It is already being published unofficially in the monthly list I compile from various sources. But this list is inevitably incomplete and can't be fully checked?

"This would be a matter for the Department of Justice as well. I haven't discussed it with them yet."

There is a gulf between our views. Yet Dermot Breen by talking to me is breaking new ground. For the first time a censor is coming out into the open.

"Why shouldn't I talk to you? I don't think that you can sit up in Harcourt Terrace and let the world go by. I think the Censor should be disposed towards talking about what he's doing, getting to know people's feelings and putting his own point of view. I don't want people feeling that I'm sitting in an ivory tower."

6 August 1972

The Dermot Breen style of censorship is beginning to emerge and the outlook is moderately liberal. It's thumbs down to

---

The July 1972 List

- Censorship of movies screened in July 1972: *Frenzy* (Appeals Board, Over 18, small cut), *King Elephant* (general, no cuts), *Steptoe & Son* (general, small cut), *Cabaret* (Over 18, small cut), *What's Up Doc?* (general, no cuts), *Plaza Suite* (Over 16, no cuts), *The Seven Magnificent Deadly Sins* (Over 16, small cut), *Kidnapped* (general, no cuts), Sitting Target (Over 18, small cut), *Powderkeg* (general, no cuts), *One Brief Summer* (Appeals Board, Over 18, cuts), *The Mephisto Waltz* (Over 18, no cuts), *Universal Soldier* (general, no cuts), *Kotch* (Appeals Board, Under 12 with Adult, small cut), *The Last Picture Show* (Over 18, no cuts), *Dirty Harry* (Over 18, no cuts), *The Touch* (Appeals Board, Over 18, cuts), *Man in the Wilderness* (Over 16, no cuts), *Embassy* (Over 16, small cuts), *The Screaming Marianne* (Over 16, cuts), *Man of Violence* (Over 16, cuts), *Count Dracula* (Over 16, no cuts), *Nashville Sound* (general, no cuts), *Saturday Night And Sunday Morning* (Appeals Board, resubmission, Over 18, no cuts), *Blood On My Hands* (Over 18, no cuts)
- Under Appeal: *Sexy Susan Knows Best, Angels Who Burn Their Wings, Such Good Friends, MOVE, Daughters of Darkness, Little Murders* (Some of these movies have been seen by the Board, but the final cut versions are not yet ready)

'sexploitation' movies like *Sexy Susan Knows Best*. Four-letter words and 'Jesus Christ' exclamations are out unless they are essential to the meaning of a scene. But top director Robert Altman's *McCabe And Mrs Miller* has been passed without cuts.

Whatever Breen does, he's prepared to it as openly as circumstances permit. As a token of this new openness, he has agreed to cooperate in the monthly lists of censorship decisions which we have been publishing unofficially since January 1971. While he is not yet prepared to volunteer information about decisions, he has agreed to check the accuracy of the list. He also has plans to meet with the movie renters shortly to discuss the feasibility of providing the public with accurate information about censorship.

13 August 1972

My detractors are breaking out into verse. Witness this (anonymous) effort:

> *Carty knows Titian,*
> *Carty's a card.*
> *Dripping with culture,*
> *Oozing with art.*
> *O Carty is arty*
> *And Carty's a hit:*
> *A connoisseur of erotica*
> *Of arses and shit.*

Well at least it's preferable to the heavy breathers who regularly ring up my wife and children on Saturday nights, well aware that I'm not in the house but at work in Middle Abbey Street putting the *Sunday Independent* to press.

What's pretentious about alluding to Titian in a movie review? Or in finding in movies an aesthetic richness comparable to that of painting, sculpture, music or literature? Literature isn't dismissed because books like *Valley of the Dolls* become best-sellers. Nobody dismisses music because of a Screaming

Lord Sutch. So why ridicule cinema as if *Carry On At Your Convenience* were the summit of its aspirations?

3 September 1972

The censorship authorities are not always to blame for cuts in movies. Proprietors of certain suburban and country cinemas are cutting prints into order to fit two features into the same programme. To prevent this, every cinema should be obliged by law to display in a prominent position in the foyer the real running times of movies being screened. If shops can be prosecuted for giving short weight and pubs for serving watered drinks, why make an exception of cinemas?

An even worse form of mutilation is that sometimes practised by distributors who, acting without the director's knowledge or consent cut certain sequences before submission to the censor in order to avoid bother. Usually this happens in London, most recently in the case of *The Samourai* and *Monte Walsh*, although there has been at least one instance this year when the Dublin distributor has been responsible.

The August 1972 List

- Censorship of movies screened in August 1972: *The Godfather* (Over 18, no cuts), *Who Is Harry Kellerman* (general, no cuts), *Chato's Land* (Over 16, small cut), *I'll Take Sweden* (Over 18, no cuts), *The Carey Treatment* (Over 18, small cut), *Cool Breeze* (Over 18, small cut), *One Is A Lovely Number* (Over 16, no cuts), *Danny Jones* (Over 18, cuts), *My Old Man's Place* (Over 18, cuts), *Lucky Luke* (general, no cuts), *Support Your Local Gunfighter* (general, no cuts), *How To Steal A Diamond* (general, no cuts), *Living Free* (general, no cuts), *Brother John* (general, no cuts), *Death Sentence* (general, no cuts), *Tarzan's Jungle* (general, no cuts)
- Under Appeal: *Decameron, Sexy Susan Knows Best, MOVE*
- Banned: *Daughters of Darkness*

1 October 1972

Stanley Kubrick's *A Clockwork Orange*, a bleak vision of a future Britain terrorised by delinquent thugs, was passed without cuts earlier this year by the British Board of Film Control. The Festival of Light lobby organised protests against its release, claiming that teenagers had been prompted by the "clockwork clock" to beat up old people. Kubrick has stood by his film, but delayed its release outside London for a year. This means that Columbia Warner will not be submitting it for censorship in Ireland: Ireland is treated as part of provincial Britain by the major distributors. Judging by the way we've mutilated movies in the past, it's hard to blame them.

Since his appointment in June, Dermot Breen has rejected only four movies (regrettably, one of these is Pasolini's *Decameron*). This has enabled the Appeals Board to clear off its backlog. Sadly all the movies passed on appeal have been cut, despite carrying Over 16 or Over 18 certificates: the most ludicrous being the cutting of Woody Allen's *Bananas*, which ought never have been banned in the first place.

The September 1972 List

- Censorship of movies screened in September 1972: *Burke and Hare* (Appeals Board, Over 18, cuts), *Impasse* (general, no cuts), *Seven Minutes* (Appeals Board, Over 18, cuts), *The Culpepper Cattle Co* (Appeals Board, Over 18, no cuts), *Straw Dogs* (Appeals Board, Over 18, cuts), *Skyjacked* (Under 12 with Adult, no cuts), *Night of the Lepus* (general, no cuts), *Blind Terror* (Over 16, no cuts), *Welcome to the Club* (Over 18, no cuts), *Billy Jack* (Over 16, no cuts), *A New Leaf* (general, no cuts), *Norwood* (Under 12 with Adult, no cuts), *A Dream Of Kings* (Over 18, no cuts), *The To Killings* (Over 18, cuts), *Where's Poppa* (Appeals Board, Over 18, cuts), *Bananas* (Appeals Board, Over 16, cuts), *The Trojan Women* (general, no cuts), *Buck and the Preacher* (general, no cuts), *The Red Circle* (general, no cuts), *Wedding Night* (Over 18, cuts)

- Under Appeal: *Straight Until Morning, MOVE, Little Murders, Sexy Susan Knows Best*

- Banned: *Decameron, Angels Who Burn their Wings*

Most of the movies so far passed by Breen have either no cuts or minimal cuts. Clearly the Appeals Board is out of touch with the new liberalism Breen is introducing. By banning so few movies, he's likely soon to make them virtually redundant. The Minister should however consider appointing a new Appeals Board more in sympathy with the times.

5 November 1972

Columbia Warner, encouraged by Dermot Breen's appointment, decided to test the water by finally submitting Ken Russell's *The Devils*. Breen was unimpressed and promptly banned it. The decision will not be appealed.

While Breen has banned only a handful of movies and is cutting fewer and fewer, unfortunately the targets for his cuts, as with the Appeals Board, are invariably Over 18 or Over 16 movies by important directors. Last month Nicholas Roeg's extraordinary *Walkabout* and Michael Ritchie's American political satire *The Candidate* suffered this fate. Why should cinema be the only art form so rigorously watered down for public consumption?

The October 1972 List

- Censorship of movies screened in October 1972: *The Candidate* (Over 16, small cuts), *BS I Love You* (Appeals Board, Over 18, cuts), *All The Right Noises* (Appeals Board, Over 18, cuts), *All Coppers Are* (Over 16, no cuts), *Evel Knievel* (general, small cut), *Shaft's Big Score* (Over 18, cuts), *A Fistful of Dynamite* (general, no cuts), *Up The Chastity Belt* (Over 16, cuts), *The Love Machine* (Over 18, small cut), *Concert For Bangladesh* (general, no cuts), *The Revengers* (general, no cuts), *Carry On Matron* (general, no cuts), *Walkabout* (Over 16, cuts), *The House That Screamed* (Over 18, no cuts), *The Hellstrom Chronicle* (general, no cuts), *Gimme Shelter* (general, no cuts), *Un Soir Un Train* (general, no cuts), *Ransom For A Dead Man* (general, no cuts)
- Under Appeal: *MOVE*
- Banned: *Straight Until Morning, Sexy Susan Knows Best*

I put the point to Breen before a crowded Economics and Commerce Society meeting at University College Dublin. Breen is unrepentant and maintains the movie directors do not deserve immunity from censorship because "many of them are perverts". Breen has shown a propensity to come out with these outrageously reactionary remarks from time to time: I can't help suspecting that he sees it as a way of placating the pro-censorship lobby. It's what Breen does as Censor rather than what he says that's likely to count in coming months.

3 December 1972

Movies are being passed so promptly by Dermot Breen that the distributors are beginning to find themselves having to queue for screening dates: there aren't enough cinemas to cope with the number of movies becoming available. When we started the monthly censorship list in January 1971, the opposite situation prevailed. So many movies were held up in censorship, the cinemas were starved for product.

Dermot Breen banned one movie last month, Richard Burton in the then infamous *Bluebeard*. He also asked Joseph Losey to tone down the bullfight sequence in *The Assassination of*

The November 1972 List

- Censorship of movies screened in November 1972: *The Pumpkin Eater* (Over 18, no cuts), *Fuzz* (Over 18, no cuts), *Hammersmith Is Out* (Over 18, cuts), *A Strange Love Affair* (Over 18, small cut), *Prime Cut* (Over 18, cuts), *The Fast Kill* (Over 18, cuts), *Up The Front* (Over 16, no cuts), *Tales from the Crypt* (Under 12 with Adult, no cuts), *Roller Derby* (general, no cuts), *Dad's Army* (general, no cuts), *McCabe And Mrs Miller* (Over 18, small cut), *Hickey And Bloggs* (Over 16, no cuts), *Dynamite Man From Glory Jail* (Under 12 with Adult, no cut), *You Are What You Eat* (general, no cuts), *Ben* (Over 16, no cuts), *Halls of Anger* (Over 16, no cuts), *Pulp* (Over 16, no cuts)
- Under Appeal: *Bluebeard, MOVE*

Trotsky, and made cuts in Peter Ustinov's *Hammersmith Is Out*, despite its Over 18 certificate.

7 January 1973

1972 has been a momentous year for Irish cinema. The dark ages of censorship, which saw either the suppression or mutilation of virtually every movie of any artistic significance, seem to be over for good. The appointment of Dermot Breen as Censor in June to succeed the late Dr Christopher Macken has introduced a process of liberalisation that is opening up Ireland to the challenge of contemporary cinema.

The December 1972 List

- Censorship of movies screened in December 1972: *Bloomfield* (general, no cuts), *What Became Of Jack and Jill* (Over 18, cuts), *Conquest of the Planet Of the Apes* (general, no cuts), *Whoever Slew Auntie Roo* (Under 12 with Adult, no cuts), *Mutiny on the Buses* (Over 16, no cuts), *Vampire Circus* (Over 18, cuts), *Weekend with a Babysitter* (Over 18, cuts), *The Hired Hand* (Appeals Board, Over 16, no cuts), *Passionate Summer* (Appeals Board, general, no cuts), *Joe Kidd* (general, no cuts), *Escape of the Birdman* (general, no cuts), *The Possession of Joel Delaney* (Over 18, cuts), *Winged Devils* (general, no cuts), *The Magnificent Seven Ride* (general, no cuts), *Zero Population Growth* (Over 18, cuts), *The Big Bounce* (Over 16, no cuts), *Red Sun* (Over 16, no cuts), *Riverrun* (general, no cuts), *Diary of a Switchboard Operator* (Appeals Board, Over 18, cuts), *The Rite* (Appeals Board, Over 18, cuts), *Alice's Adventures in Wonderland* (general, no cuts), *Napoleon and Samantha* (general, no cuts), *Black Belly of the Tarantula* (Over 18, no cuts), *Weekend Murders* (Over 16, no cuts), *The War Between Men And Women* (general, no cuts), *False Witness* (general, no cuts), *The Jerusalem File* (general, no cuts), *Catlow* (general, no cuts), *Every Little Crook and Nanny* (general, no cuts), *Bunny O'Hare* (Under 12, cut), *Fear in the Night* (Under 12, no cuts), *Lady Caroline Lamb* (Under 12, no cuts), *Doomwatch* (general, no cuts), *On Any Sunday* (general, no cuts)
- Under Appeal: *MOVE*
- Banned: *Bluebeard*

Nothing more dramatically demonstrates his impact than the fact that this time last year at least twenty-six movies, banned by the Censor, were awaiting appeal. Now there is only one. The number of movies sent for appeal in 1972 almost halved from 103 to 57, but the more significant figure, revealed in our unofficial monthly list of censorship decisions, is that only 5 of the 57 movies going to appeal come from the period since Breen took over as Censor.

The data for 1972 reveals little apparent change in the policy of cutting movies already restricted to adult audiences, although the emphasis now seems to be on language rather than visuals. Of the eighty-four movies cut, seventy-two carried adult certificates, fifty-five were Over 18, sixteen were Over 16. However Breen has made cuts in only twenty-three — often small dialogue cuts — of the forty-four movies he restricted to adult audiences, a dramatic improvement. Among the Over 18 movies he didn't cut were *The Last Picture Show, The Godfather* and *The Hospital.*

So far the Appeals Board doesn't seem to have got the message. During December they bowdlerised the final scene of Ingmar Bergman's *The Rite* and removed chunks of Dusan Majavejev's *Diary of a Switchboard Operator.* But with virtually none of Breen's decisions going to appeal, their capacity to do harm from now on is happily curtailed.

Since his appointment, Breen, while prevented by Department of Justice bureaucracy from volunteering information about his decisions, has been prepared to confirm or deny information in the monthly unofficial list published in the *Sunday Independent.* He has promised to consult the renters in an attempt to devise some way of making information available from official sources.

POSTSCRIPT

The monthly list of censorship decisions continued to appear in the *Sunday Independent* until 1974. By then the original need for it — to undermine a reactionary and secretive censorship system by exposure and ridicule — had passed. Irish film censorship had come into line with that in other Western countries.

In some ways the Irish system, operated reasonably, was superior to that prevailing in the UK. Once a movie was granted a certificate in Ireland, it had the full protection of the law. No other public body pressure group could prevent it being screened commercially. Whereas in the UK local authorities and watch committees still acted as censors in addition to the British Board of Film Control.

Dermot Breen remained true to his promise of openness. We became something of a double act at debates throughout the country, Breen defending his decisions and me challenging them. At times he would feel obliged to reassure the Catholic right. Proclaiming his great love of cinema to Cork Rotary Club in 1974, he reiterated his determination to protect it from the "many insidious elements in our midst who are attempting to corrupt our society by upsetting many of our long-established institutions and traditions." Some of these groups "were demanding and pressing for the removal of censorship of films, and indeed of all the things which were considered decent in accordance with the normal standards of living in a well ordered society." He would not tolerate "masochistic, psychopathic and megalomaniac directors" who were bent on manufacturing scenes that "have no place in cinema, let alone in a civilised, intelligent society like ours".

What was important was that he was delivering this tirade in public, and it was open to me or anyone else to challenge him. Meanwhile his actual decisions gave the lie to his seemingly reactionary stance. Only nineteen censorship decisions were appealed in 1973, compared with 103 in 1971. Only a few of these were controversial: the banning of Kubrick's *A Clockwork Orange* and Fellini's *Roma*. *Roma* was passed on appeal but Fellini, alerted by me, refused to agree to the cuts.

Although we stopped publishing the censorship list after 1974, I continued to monitor Breen's decisions. Occasionally I'd feel obliged to challenge a decision, but the war as such was over.

If Irish audiences were being denied a chance to see serious cinema, the fault was no longer so much censorship as the failure of renters and exhibitors to programme anything other than mainstream Hollywood and UK product. Subtitled movies, other than the work of a few big names like Bergman, Fellini and Antonioni, were virtually confined to film societies.

Cannes Film Festival each year was a reminder of just how isolated Irish audiences were becoming. Virtually none of the movies highlighted there — other than American or British — ever reached Ireland.

In September 1973 a group of us met in Wolf Mankowitz's flat in Ballsbridge to explore the possibility of launching an art-house cinema in Dublin, run by by Joey Malkinson of the Vintage Film Club. We formed a provisional committee of Hugh Leonard, Lynn Redgrave, Dan O'Herlihy, Robert Bolt, Fergus Linehan, John Boorman, Wolf, Joey and myself. Charlie Haughey promised £1,000 to get the project started. Unfortunately planning difficulties prevented us finding suitable premises — the intitial venue in Blackrock was too small and too out of the way.

The Project Arts Centre later took up the idea. Situated behind the Olympia Theatre in East Essex Street, it had been set up as an artists co-op in 1969 by twenty-four-year-old Colm O Briain, and the two Sheridan brothers, Jim and Peter. The Sheridans, still in their early twenties, were already theatre veterans, having been blooded as writers and actors while still children in their father's local theatre group in Sherriff Street. They had built up an ensemble of players that included Neil Jordan, who had just set up a writers co-op of his own to publish his first collection of short stories, *Night In Tunisia*: it was lavishly praised by Sean O'Faolain as a breakthrough in Irish fiction.

Project up to now had operated as an experimental theatre space and gallery. O'Briain had always intended it to embrace cinema as well, in keeping with its policy of promoting the interrelationship of the arts. In January 1975 he was appointed director of a revamped Arts Council. One of his first decisions was to widen the powers of the Council to include cinema, which had not been considered an art form by the previous Council. Project formed a film cooperative in September 1975 and invited me to join its programme committee run by Ruth Riddick. We opened with the Irish premiere of Rainer Werner Fassbinder's *Fear Eats The Soul*, and followed with Wim Wenders' *The Goalkeeper's Fear of the Penalty* and several of the movies that had impressed me at Cannes — notably Jean Eustache's *The Mother and the Prostitute*. At the same time, the Arts Council helped set up the International Film Theatre, a club cinema featuring world films.

Project's ambition was not just to provide access to new continental cinema but to provide a model for would-be Irish filmmakers. O'Briain was particularly impressed by the achievement of German directors like Fassbinder, Wenders and Herzog, whose low-budget movies on contemporary themes had been financed in co-production deals with German television networks. RTE, with whom the Sheridans, Jordan and other Project members were already involved, could perhaps fulfil a similar role in jump-starting Irish film production.

CHAPTER FOUR

THE SORCERER AND HIS APPRENTICE

1

The Domino Effect

The John Huston-inspired Film Bill, shelved in 1970, had been an attempt to impose a film industry from scratch before any of the elements were in place that would have given it a chance to succeed. The elements needed to make it work just were not in the power of the Dail to deliver.

Although it's common practice to talk of the production of movies as an industry, movies are in fact something much more intangible. The production of kettles or ballpoint pens can be accurately termed as an industry. Movies on the other hand are an unlikely combination of commerce and art. No matter what the deal nor how shrewd the marketing, they ultimately depend on unpredictable human creative factors.

The actual production of movies is an industrial process, but movies themselves, flawed or crass though they often may be, come out of nowhere. John Boorman has described their production as an act of turning "money into light". They are hazardous one-offs that originate in a flash of inspiration, however banal. There's never any telling beforehand whether they will have any commercial potential whatsover.

Nobody can make a movie alone. Movies are the most cooperative of all art forms. Yet they ultimately depend on sheer individuality.

If the talent is in place to create movies, then government support in the form of grants, loans, tax-break and facilities can be a crucial catalyst. If it's not, it's money down the drain.

In 1970 nobody could have argued that Ireland had this immediate potential. There were a handful of documentary directors of some imagination: Patrick Carey had won an Oscar as a second-unit cameraman, Louis Marcus was nominated for an Oscar for one of his shorts, Kieran Hickey had just made *Faithful Departed*, an imaginative evocation of Joyce's Dublin inspired by rare photographs from the Lawrence collection in the National Library.

There was probably a small pool of technicians working abroad who might be lured back. But there were no potential Irish feature directors waiting in the wings. Nor was there any government awareness of the creative potential of cinema. Fianna Fail saw a film industry primarily as an export industry based on the output of international productions that would use Ireland as a film facility and location.

The eventual belated emergence of a viable Irish film industry was a chance coming together of people who happened to be in the right place at the right time. It was like dominos knocking together, except that nobody really recognised the dominos for what they were until they all fell into place.

Still, as a film critic and arts editor, I was lucky enough to be in a position to comment on this gradual unfolding of a native film culture. What follows is a frame-by-frame — and sometimes flash-back account — of the major characters as they begin to emerge, as seen through a series of profiles and interviews that I did with them over the past two decades.

Let's begin with the sorcerer and his apprentice. Then call in the RTE maverick who opted out and the news editor who dreamt of becoming a mogul. For funding look not to Ireland but to a revolution in British television. Throw in a poet who as a result of a freak political deal suddenly found himself with millions to spend on the arts. Bring back a couple of exiles with something to prove. Add some surprise Oscars and follow up with generous tax-breaks. What you get is Hollywood on the Liffey: Part Two...

2

The Sorcerer

John Boorman only has to will an earthquake and Ethiopia caves in. Never mind that it's just a miniature set built by Richard MacDonald for *The Heretic*. Cameras will make it seem terrifyingly real. Creating movies for Boorman has always being a kind a sorcery, a chance to play Merlin.

It's a balmy summer evening in 1977. His wife Christel has prepared a salad dinner in a large room overlooking the river that meanders through their valley in Annamoe in the Wicklow mountains. A neighbour Garech Browne has dropped in from Lugalla with the cartoonist Nick Robinson and his wife, Mary, a brilliant young lawyer who challenged the secrecy of film censorship in a debate in the Seanad.

Boorman and Christel found Annamoe by chance. They were looking for a holiday cottage in 1970, heard about an auction and walked out owners of The Glebe, an old stone presbytery. He sees it as his sanctuary from the ravages of the film industry. "When I'm not filming, it's where I am to be found."

Annamoe has also become a home away from home for many of Boorman's Hollywood friends. So much so that he has had an extra bed put in to accommodate burly Lee Marvin, star of *Point Blank*, the thriller that lured Boorman to the States in 1967.

Sean Connery has been a regular since playing the avenging Zed in the sci-fi parable *Zardoz*, which Boorman shot on location in the surrounding hills in 1973. Charlotte Rampling, too. Not to mention Marcello Mastroianni, who made his English-language debut in Boorman's *Leo the Last* (which ran foul of the Irish censor), and Burt Reynolds and Jon Voight from *Deliverance*, Boorman's chilling riposte to the Hollywood cult of redemption through violence.

Moving to Ireland gave Boorman a feeling of coming home. His family were originally Dutch, fleeing persecution in the Inquisition to build dykes on the West coast of England. Boorman's grandfather, who married an Irish woman named Fitzpatrick, invented and mass-produced the first washing machine: when Boorman left school he set him up with a few laundromats.

There is also Celtic blood on Boorman's mother's side, to which he attributes a fascination with myth that underlies his movies. "Cinema is the repository of myth," he says.

Although born a Protestant, his mother sent him to school with the Jesuits, where Father John McGuire ("almost a second father") encouraged him to write. He read widely and became hooked on the Arthurian legends and the idea of the quest for the Holy Grail. His films in many ways are reworkings of this medieval myth. All his heroes feel impelled to undertake journeys from which they emerge reborn. "Like a film director making a movie," he says, wryly.

To Father McGuire's disappointment, Boorman left school at sixteen — he suffered from dyslexia and found studying difficult — to become a clapper boy at nearby Shepperton Studios. "As children we were always hanging around, watching pictures being made," he says. He became involved in BBC Radio's 'Under 20 Review', covering the arts. He was in at the start of commercial television, running Southern TV's 'Day by Day' current affairs programme, then producing the weekly 'Arena' show, hosted by Anthony Wedgewood Benn.

With Huw Weldon's backing he created 'The Newcomers' for the launch of BBC 2 in 1964, a series of documentaries which were the first to identify what became known as Swinging London. One episode featured a party with many of Boorman's friends, including the playwrights Tom Stoppard, Charles Wood and Peter Nichols. "We probably invented the Swinging Sixties, but we never had any of the fun. We just made it up."

He'd become impatient with the limitation of documentary film-making. "My documentaries gradually became more dramatised. I found it frustrating to be on the outside, not to be able to enter people. It was always frustrating that the most important things happened when you weren't there."

His debut movie *Catch Us If You Can* in 1966, scripted by Nichols, gave an imaginative fictional dimension to the rock band genre. MGM liked it and offered him *Point Blank*, a script in which Lee Marvin had shown interest. "Hollywood was in crisis. With the shock of TV, the whole studio system was collapsing. Everyone was looking to Swinging London for new life. We were the new raiders."

Boorman met Marvin on the set of *The Dirty Dozen* and they immediately took to each other, so much so that Marvin transferred all his approvals over casting, script and crew to Boorman. That way Boorman was able to make *Point Blank* his own way, without studio interference, brilliantly stretching the possibilities of the thriller genre and giving rein to his growing distrust of realism. "The most pretentious film-making is realism. Because it's pretentious for anyone to suggest that they can recreate reality."

Boorman invents isolated worlds governed exclusively by their own rules, rather than attempting to duplicate what's there. In *Point Blank* it was the American underworld: he deployed colour expressionistically to evoke the moods of the characters. *Hell in the Pacific*, again with Marvin, had two enemies marooned together on a remote Pacific island. *Zardoz* existed entirely in a fantasy future dominated by women.

In *Deliverance*, four friends on a weekend canoeing holiday are suddenly plunged into an elemental backwoods culture of distrust and cruelty. It's shot with a heightened realism that is in fact totally manufactured. The startling immediacy of the sound of the rushing cataract is achieved with a Moog synthesiser. The dialogue is all looped.

Part of the attraction of *The Heretic* is that it offers the possibility of destroying reality in order to create it. "I was attracted to it because it was inspired by Theilhard de Chardin. It's about the possibility of spiritual evolution, of minds coming together. It's a kind of metaphysical chiller." Showing his distaste for naturalism, the entire movie is shot in shades of amber: blues and greens are eliminated because they would have been too cheerful.

Like John Huston, Boorman never misses an opportunity to locate his movies in Ireland. Although most of *The Heretic*, the $14 million sequel to *The Exorcist*, is being filmed in Burbank, California, on the biggest exterior sets built in a studio since the golden era of the 1930s, Boorman has contrived to do all the model work sequences as well as the editing and dubbing at Ardmore Studios.

It's meant defying nature and swarming Ireland with locusts. The locusts have been brought into Ireland individually packed in tiny cellophane containers. To avoid the danger of the pests proliferating, the health authorities only permit males to be imported. So thousands of locusts had to be submitted to rigorous sex tests by customs authorities.

"Something of a change from scrutinising *The Catcher in the Rye* to see if it's obscene," I remark.

Suspecting that the reason the Irish have never been able to make movies might be that they spend too much time talking about it and that reports, commissions and abortive bills in the Dail have become an excuse for putting off decisions, Boorman persuaded the new Inter-Party coalition Government, elected in 1973, and in particular Minister for Industry and Commerce Justin Keating, a former RTE producer, to set up a company to run Ardmore Studios with himself as chairman: the bankrupt studios had just been bought by RTE. Ardmore became the

National Film Studios in 1975, run by Sheamus Smith, former editor of RTE's current affairs programme 'Seven Days'.

"The real breakthrough was in 1974 when film workers got sufficiently organised to insist on RTE commercials being made here by Irish film technicians and producers instead of in Britain. This meant that there is a regular flow of work at Ardmore. It has enabled workers to cut their teeth in film-making."

But having a studio, even if, as Boorman hopes, it evolves into a sort of movie centre, complete with comprehensive training facilities for apprentice workers, will not itself put Ireland on the movie map. Unless a Film Board is set up, with sufficient funds to stimulate various forms of production, including experimental work in animation and video, Ardmore is likely to remain little more than a convenient facility for international productions.

"Justin has been terrific. He's passionately interested in the whole thing. But the Government haven't come up with the money they said would be available. They have reneged."

Boorman gives me a copy of his script for *Merlin*, which he hopes to film after *The Heretic*. It's a project he's wanted to tackle since the 1960s. "It's a story of lost magic and remembered magic, echoes of a golden age that we somehow lost. It's a link with a time when men were greater than they are now. I spent the whole summer of 1975 writing it. It was an immense effort and I was totally exhausted. The thought of filming it was really daunting. So I'm doing *The Heretic* in between to get a distance from it.

"Now I have come back to it and look at it in a much more dispassionate way. I can look at it as a director, something outside of myself."

1975-77

3

The Apprentice

Neil Jordan is sipping a glass of red rioja wine. "When I worked in the wine cellar of Fortnum and Mason, we'd drink vintage champagne like stout," he says.

We're sitting at a table in the front room of my home in Goatstown, just outside Dublin. It's early autumn in 1978. He gets up and walks to the window, then sits down again humming some tune. He just can't seem to stay still. He keeps breaking off in mid-sentence, as if his thoughts are running ahead of his words and then coming back to interrupt them.

His job at Fortnums in Piccadilly was to pack orders for celebrities like Michael Caine and Otto Preminger. "You had this sense of being in contact with those who were in contact with them.

"The Queen used come in every now and then and the attendants, in their posh morning suits, most of them were gay, would say: "Oh, isn't her pink just gorgeous."

Eventually Jordan gave up taking part-time jobs, and devoted all his time to writing. "Unemployment can be a great blessing. It should be compulsory for three years, like army service."

He persuaded Colm O'Briain at the Arts Council to give Des Hogan and himself a grant of £900 to set up the Irish Writers Co-Operative in 1976, despite the fact that they had no experience in publishing.

Its main purpose initially was to publish their own short stories — Hogan's *The Ikon Maker* and Jordan's *Night in Tunisia*.

"Des and I had been sending work off together to London. Publishers wrote back saying that normally they would have published us but they couldn't because of cutbacks in their fiction lists. "

Sean O'Faolain welcomed *Night in Tunisia* as "one of the most remarkable stories I have read in Irish story-telling since, or indeed before Joyce."

Now two years later the Co-Op has established itself, together with Poolbeg Press and Blackstaff in Belfast, as a launching pad for new Irish writing, with sales of first fiction averaging 2,000 copies. "If English publishers sell even 1,000 with a first novel, they think they're doing very well."

Jordan quit UCD in 1970 to travel around Europe for a year, giving English classes in Spain to support his writing. "I didn't fit in at university. They told me their function was merely to teach, that the English department had nothing to do with creativity. They were so busy learning the language in retrospect — building up the critical methodology to deal with Beckett, Proust and Joyce — that they couldn't respond to language as it was being created."

He taught for a while as a supply teacher, first in Dublin and then in London, taking classes when other teachers didn't turn up. "Our schools are much more violent. Dublin vocational schools are really deprived. I remember taking the art teacher's class but the headmaster wouldn't let me use the art equipment. No paper, no paints, no anything. I was just supposed to sit there keeping the kids quiet and stopping them breaking the windows."

For a while he played saxophone with a rock group and did some street theatre with the Children's T Company, putting on entertainments in schools and at street corners, opening children's eyes to the possibilities of drama.

He'd studied classical guitar and saxophone as a schoolboy. His father, who was a teacher, played the violin. "We'd play duets together and go to symphony concerts. But at a certain age

I ceased to do that sort of stuff. I was into rock'n'roll and jazz. I remember feeling rather sad. I didn't want to go to concerts with him any more but I knew he wanted me to go. He'd leave tickets on the mantelpiece and I'd never take them."

While performing as a musician on an RTE children's programme, he met the show's presenter Jim Sheridan, who was also studying at UCD. Sheridan and his brother Peter were involved in the student theatre company Slot, and Jordan joined them, touring Chicago in 1972. They'd also joined with Colm O'Briain to set up the Project Arts Centre, through which Jordan became involved in Children's T company, writing sketches.

All the images that had haunted him since childhood began to find form in short stories. He'd read a lot as a boy, in between painting: his mother and grandmother both painted, and for a long while he thought he'd be a painter, like his sister Eithne, who already has had an exhibition at Project. "I'd read anything that was lying around the house. I was obsessed with Yeats. It's a lovely world to get into. It's magnificent to be Irish and to have some sort of kinship with him."

Since his father was a teacher, there were long family holidays by the sea every summer. He was born in Sligo in 1950, but moved to Clontarf when he was two and used go to Bray for holidays with his mother's family. At Belgrove National School he was taught for a while by John McGahern, who was later sacked.

Many of the stories in *Night in Tunisia* are about growing up: nearly all are filled with a pervasive sense of the sea.

"There has always been an image — whether a memory or an emotional object with associations —at the centre of my approach to writing," he says. Perhaps that's why he is drawn increasingly to cinema. "The sensual immediacy of thinking strictly in images is very refreshing," he says.

He seems to enjoy the challenge of crossing over into other media. BBC have just performed his radio play *Miracles* and *Miss Langan*, in which a young teacher just out of a seminary meets an older woman who is his cultural opposite. There are hopes that RTE will film it next year. BBC have commissioned a TV script based on *Night In Tunisia*.

Perhaps Jordan will end up in movies. But now at twenty-eight nearly all his time is devoted to finishing his first novel. He's working on it every day in the National Library. "There's a great stillness there, especially in the summer. Nobody to disturb you, except coming up to the exams."

Already married — he met Vivienne at college, and they have a three year old daughter Sarah — he has been enabled to do this with a £2,500 writer's bursary from the Arts Council. "Writers don't have to emigrate any more," he says.

1978

4

The Would-Be Mogul

Blonde hair rippling sensuously over her shoulders, Miss Finland languishes in her wicker chair while a make-up girl tones her lipstick and a lighting man checks the exposure readings.

Behind a cluster of lamps and cameras, a stage-hand is carefully ironing stacks of pink, blue and yellow tissues.

The red warning light comes on.

Another commercial is ready to shoot at the National Film Studios in Ardmore — a Kleenex advertisement for Finnish cinemas. "Commercials like this are our bread and butter," says studio boss Sheamus Smith. "Feature films will be the jam."

Since Ardmore reopened just over a year ago in August 1975, the commercials have been coming in on an average of three a week, mainly from RTE and UTV. But because of the failure of the Government to follow through on its commitment to a comprehensive package of tax-breaks and production finance, there hasn't been much jam.

"A revolving fund of five million dollars is needed," says Smith. "It could be raised partly from the Exchequer and partly from financing companies with government guarantees. The important thing to remember in cinema financing is that you don't necessarily need the money, but you do have to be able to show that you have access to it."

About a third of *Victor Frankenstein*, produced by Calvin Floyd with finance from the Swedish Film Institute, was serviced by the studio. And Marty Feldman's *Beau Geste* has just moved out after several weeks on location at Adare and Kilmainham.

The actual shooting time it spent at Ardmore was six days. "What people don't appreciate is that there is more to a picture than shooting," says Smith. "It needs the studio for editing, for sound transfers, for dubbing and for offices. Whether *Beau Geste* was filming in Adare or Kilmainham didn't really matter. We were servicing it here."

Although the crews for *Victor Frankenstein* and *Beau Geste* were brought in, Smith believes this will change as the word gets out about the availability of trained Irish technicians. He is sceptical of the claim that Ireland doesn't need Ardmore, that it would be more realistic to spend money directly on Irish films which could be shot on location without studios.

"That's unreal. Pictures have to be based somewhere. They are a whole infrastructure. Even if you didn't shoot anything on the stages, you'd still need a studio."

Although substantial sums have been spent re-equipping the studios, there is a distinct air of marking time about the place.

Yet a few miles down the dual carriageway at Donnybrook, hundreds of thousands of feet of film are being shot every year. Ireland already has a *de facto* film industry. It's called Radio Telifis Eireann.

"You name it, we shoot it," says senior cameraman Stuart Hetherington. "Every moment we're on the air, there has to be something on that screen. This week we have crews in Holland, Italy and the United States, where Mike Murphy is completing a series of six one-hour programmes. By the end of this year we'll have eleven complete crews operating in the programme area."

Within RTE there is now an impressive pool of technical, writing and producing talent that makes it realistic to talk in terms of Irish-produced feature films.

Most of the leading film-makers in the UK and the US graduated to movies through television, directors like John Boorman, Arthur Penn, John Frankenheimer, Sidney Lumet and Ken Russell. There's no reason why, given the right stimulus through the introduction of a Film Bill, the same thing shouldn't happen in Ireland. In fact it's already beginning to happen.

Stuart Hetherington is giving the lead with his camerawork on Joseph Strick's *Portrait of the Artist*. "Here's a movie that proves once and for all that the technical and acting ability to make movies are here. All that's needed is a guy like Strick to make it happen."

Shooting *Portrait* literally meant going back to school for Hetherington. One of the locations was Belvedere College, which he quit at sixteen for a chance to work as an office boy at Ardmore Studios. "My father went to the Rector and said, 'Listen, he's been offered a job in that lunatic bin, will you take him back if it doesn't work out?'" Hetherington shrugs: "I didn't have to go back until now."

Focusing on John Gielgud in full flow delivering the notorious hell-fire sermon, it was as if Hetherington had never left. "It was as convincing as anything I'd heard when I was a fourteen-year-old on retreat."

Hetherington was thrown in at the deep end at Ardmore. "I spent a week with Freddie Young getting background shots for *The Gorgon* at Colliemore Harbour. I was on the camera crew shooting *Shake Hands With The Devil, The Siege of Sidney Street* and *A Terrible Beauty*. I was working with people I'd heard about in magazines. No amount of money could buy that experience."

When Telefis Eireann was launched in 1962, he was one of the first to be signed on. "Telefis has taken over where Ardmore left off in the early 1960s," he says. "It has given some sort of hope to the people who believe in the possibility of Irish feature movies."

Among Hetherington's award-winning drama productions have been the Eugence McCabe *Victims* series and Brian MacLoughlin's *A Day in the Life of Martin Cluxton*.

"It's the best possible training ground for cinema because it is practical," he says. "Schedules have to be observed. You don't think in the big Hollywood style. At RTE the pennies always have to be counted. You get used to getting around a problem in the simplest possible way."

Joseph Strick filmed *Portrait* with the same discipline, shooting it originally in 16mm. "It made the whole operation so much lighter and mobile. You could do anything with the darn thing. When we later blew it up into 35mm, it picked up that little bit of grain, but so what, it's supposed to be 1900, and that way we added the period atmosphere.

"When you think of film-making on that modest scale, and with that inventiveness, anything becomes possible."

1976-77

5

The Maverick Who Went West

Connemara is on the very edge of Europe, a strange and different place. There's nothing between it and America. Coral beaches with translucent water lace its hundreds of desolate inlets. Often the only building on the bleak mountain slopes is an overgrown stone famine cottage, deserted from the last century. Road signs are only in Irish because most of the villages don't have English names.

"It's isolated by its language," says Bob Quinn, as he works at the editing desk in Cinegael, the movie co-op he set up at Carraroe, in the heart of the Connemara Gaeltacht. Outside the mountains are shrouded in mist in the winter of 1976. "It's like a foreign country. Coming here was the equivalent of going to France. I'll always be a stranger there and I'm a stranger here too."

He's at pains to make clear that he didn't resign his job as a producer and director with RTE in 1969. "I literally walked out of the place. The distinction is important. My departure broke all their polite conventions."

He was drawn to Carraroe with his wife Helen and small children because "it didn't have the imitative tendencies of urban areas. Everything in Dublin is second-hand. It's a provincial city. There is very little original thought that hasn't been stimulated by something outside the country. Carraroe at least has the insulation from the American/English world, which nauseates me because of its commercial density."

He didn't come to Carraroe with the intention of making films. He wrote and made crafts — batiks and lino cuts. "I was selling toffee apples to make a living."

But, perhaps inevitably, he had the outrageous idea of forming a film and video tape unit. Cinegael initially produced video tapes for screening on closed circuit television around the village halls. Quinn also started a film club. " The most successful movie we've shown was Bruce Lee's kung fu epic *Enter The Dragon*. There were even queues for it. Whereas people walked out of Robert Flaherty's *Man of Aran*."

He admits there's an incongruity in bringing to Connemara ikons of the commercialism he walked out of in Dublin. "The corners have been knocked off me," he says. "I've become a little more realistic about what it is possible to do. I've stopped thinking in terms of what is good for people."

In collaboration with cameraman Joe Comerford, an independent film-maker who worked with him in RTE, he has now launched into feature production with *Caoineadh Airt Ui Laoire*, which he wrote, produced, directed, shot, recorded and edited at Cinegael. Although finance came from Gardiner Street Sinn Fein, he had a completely free hand.

Quite apart from the unlikely conditions under which it was created, it is an extraordinary work of cinema, rich in spontaneous humour, vibrating with the authentic sound and feel of the West, the sound and feel of Ireland.

Its form is both simple and effective: a movie within a movie. The English playwright John Arden — who like Quinn, opted out of the cultural mainstream to live in Connemara — is shown trying to organise a local drama presentation of the story of Ui Laoire, one of the Wild Geese who returned from the continent and died rather than surrender the horse he was prohibited from owning under the anti-Catholic Penal Laws. The distinction between past and present is continuously confused. The actor playing Ui Laoire keeps becoming Ui Laoire. Arden personifies the English Ascendancy, yet the analogy is never exaggerated.

We're not tricked into forgetting that we're watching a movie. The actors are in a way conducting a dialogue with themselves and with the audience. As Ui Laoire absurdly rides off to confront his English tormentor, he represents 700 years of fighting for independence. "What I want to know is, does he have a mandate?" a Northern voice demands. "This senseless violence will achieve nothing," wails a clergyman.

Caoineadh Airt Ui Laoire plainly shows that movies in Ireland are possible even without Government support or studio facilities. It has its faults — technical inelegancies, if you like — but it is sustained by a belief in itself which is totally contagious.

Shamefully it has been refused a release in any Irish cinema. Its premiere instead took place at Project Arts Centre in Dublin in a season that also included Carlos Saura's *Peppermint Frappe* and Wim Wenders *Alice In the Cities*. It has since been screened at the Cork Film Festival and also invited to Pesaro, perhaps the most progressive festival in Europe and one particularly concerned with innovations in cinema. Rome's *Il Messagiero* critic acclaimed it as a moving experience in which the harshness of the Irish sounds was matched by the tough, inelegant images.

None of these achievements seems to have impressed the Department of the Gaeltacht. Cinegael have received none of the £30,000 spent by the Department on filming — although they are the only film unit based in the Gaeltacht.

Undaunted, Quinn has just finished a movie on stone carving in collaboration with the composer Roger Doyle, who specialises in found music. "I wanted to define prosaic images with strange and unusual sounds."

Next spring he hopes to film a screenplay written by a Carna farmer who took part in a movie course at Cinegael. "It will be a far cry from the nice tourist image you see about Connemara, the pretty postcards and the donkeys. It will show the very tough people who live there."

It's the kind of de-mythification television could be dealing with — but seldom does. And that was the reason Quinn walked out of RTE.

"RTE is in the terrible position of being a public service and at the same time being forced to pay its way through commercials".

"This straitjacket has destroyed all possibility of TV ever becoming anything. It short-circuits all the efforts of the best people there, because they know when it comes to the crunch they're not going to be able to say what they want to say because of commercial considerations."

Quinn claims, and it's an argument he propounded with another former RTE producer, Lelia Doolan, in their book *Stand Up and Be Counted,* that with certain honourable exceptions — he instances the Eugene McCabe trilogy *Victims* — RTE contents itself with filming beautiful productions. "They're the worst of both worlds. They're not really making films and they're not really making television. It's a retreat from immediacy, a form of playing safe, a form of negative selections."

Quinn's exile in Connemara is by no means total. He has filmed in Canada and makes frequent sallies to Dublin, where he worked for Joe Comerford filming *Down the Corner*, a story by teacher Noel McFarlane about young people in working class Ballyfermot. "There was opposition from local people at first because RTE and BBC programmes had shown only what was worst about Ballyfermot. We reaped the harvest. But gradually common sense prevailed and people realised we weren't going to do the dirty on them."

1976-77

6

Going It Alone

While the National Film Studios continue to wait in frustration
for a Film Bill that still remains no more than a promise, already
in 1977 a makeshift *de facto* independent film industry is
struggling into being.

Down The Corner has been produced by Art O'Briain through
Ballyfermot Arts Workshop. "We wanted to get away from the
idea that cinema had to be glitter. It should instead be accessible
to everyone. Pictures should come out of the experiences of the
audience that will see them. We're pointing the way to the kind
of pictures that can be made in Ireland. I'm confident such
pictures could recoup their low budgets from Irish audiences
alone. Pleasing foreign audiences should be thought of only as
a secondary consideration."

Down The Corner was financed with £4,000 from Dublin
Corporation, £5,000 from RTE and £4,000 from the Arts
Council. "But we had to go to the British Film Institute for the
completion money," says director Joe Comerford. "Nobody here
could come up with the final £7,000."

Comerford, with Bob Quinn as cameraman and Cathal Black
as his assistant, used an almost entirely Ballyfermot cast for the
story about schoolboys robbing orchards. "The boys had to get
up at six o'clock every morning when we were shooting and then
go to school. Yet they never let us down."

Comerford started making movies ("Super 8 stuff that nobody
sees") as a design student in the National College of Art in the
1960s, a time of revolt when the students, taking their cue from

124

Europe, sought to overthrow archaic teaching structures. For his final diploma he made *Entigon*, a fourteen-minute portrait of an old man and his violation of a young woman, which was shown on RTE. He worked there briefly before quitting to film *Withdrawal*, a stark look at a drug addict's struggle to survive.

He was unhappy with it as it was originally screened on RTE and commissioned James Brennan, whose first novel *Seamen* had been published by Irish Writers Co-Op, to write a remake. "The material, based on David Chapman's book, had been written in a very literary way. I'd had a sort of nagging thing about it for years, a feeling that there was stuff in the off-cuts that should have been in the original.

"I began working on it again, thinking I'd re-edit it. But I realised it wasn't simply a question of changing the picture. The basic structure had to be tackled.

"Jimmy was just the writer I needed. He has a marvellous ability to write straight to pictures. I didn't show him the original version or let him read the screenplay. We just looked over all the footage, talked about different possible directions it might take and then he'd go away and write to that brief.

"Originally I'd thought of getting an actor to speak the narration, but Jimmy finished up doing that too."

"What I'm trying to do is to combine documentary with narrative form," he says.

1977

7

The Shock Of The Un-Irish

Reading James Joyce is like taking a crash course in cinematic language. "He looked at the world in a cinematic way before cinema had really been invented," says Kieran Hickey. Hickey is a South Circular Road Dubliner, who was reared on Saturday matinees. "Joyce wasn't offered to me as a boy. I wasn't taught about him at school. He was looked upon as an embarrassment and a scandal."

Joyce's offence was to offer a view of reality that contradicted the official myths about Irishness articulated so quaintly by De Valera in his celebrated 1943 St Patrick's Day broadcast. The rural idyll of comely maidens dancing at the crossroads was dinned into Hickey at school. To be truly Irish was to speak Irish and live in a thatched cottage in the West. Urban life was in some way un-Irish.

Dubliners and *Portrait of the Artist*, which Hickey discovered as a teenager, were a liberation. "It was immensely reassuring to know a writer who understood what urban life was about. I reached out to Joyce because he related to my own experience. What I had in front of me in his work was there in my everyday life. We've grown up with eyes which he had before any of us.

"Something as simple as that was in its way more shattering than any other statement he could have made: the realisation that there could be art in naming the Wellington Monument, Sydney Parade, the Sandymount tram, Downses cake shop and Williamses jam."

Coming upon a reality in the written word that he recognised and could identify with was a stimulus to Hickey to find his own way of giving it expression.

Patricia Hutchins' James Joyce's Ireland, which he bought with fifteen shillings saved up from pocket money, led to his discovery in the National Library of the little-known Lawrence collection which contained over 40,000 newsreel-like photographs of the Dublin of Joyce's youth.

"They conveyed this frozen sense of time. They recorded visually the images of Dublin Joyce had taken away in his mind and in his heart and later drawn on in his writing. They give us a glimpse of the Dublin that had become fixed in his memory."

These photographs were to become the source of Hickey's first movie Faithful Departed on his return to Dublin in the 1960s after studying at the London Film School. His camera zoomed in on the random detail of street life to bring alive that day in 1904 when time stood still for Joyce. The evocative power of the images was heightened by using songs and arias like 'M'appari', 'The Young May Moon' and 'I Dreamt I Dwelt in Marble Halls' which recur in Ulysses.

Although Faithful Departed was chosen to represent Ireland at the 1969 Paris Biennale, Hickey had only been able to film it with the backing of the BBC: there was no support for him in Ireland, an irony that Joyce would have wryly appreciated.

"If I have learned to look at my own society with any clarity, it is because of Joyce," says Hickey.

With Colm O'Briain now running the Arts Council, film-makers like Hickey, Comerford and Quinn are being brought in out of the cold.

One of O'Briain's first initiatives was to inaugurate an annual film script award. In 1977 it went to Quinn for Poitin. Hickey won it the following year for his forty-five-minute feature Exposure.

The first and last shots of Exposure are blank: in between we are exposed to subtle shifts in a relationship between three surveyors and a woman photographer whose lives briefly come together and part in a dreary hotel in the West of Ireland.

The woman, movingly played by Catherine Schell, is foreign: exposure to her moral freedom (she turns out to be married, but divorced) and alien sensuality undermines momentarily the forced male camaraderie and repressed passion of the men (who could, if the audience choose, be taken to personify the plight of the Irish male in a matriarchal society).They are TP McKenna, hen-pecked and alcoholic, in whom all feeling has long ago withered; Niall O'Brien, ringing a uninterested wife every night, already beginning to feel himself being sucked into the same living grave; and Bosco Hogan, the bachelor, a reminder of what the other two once were, as he has his brief fling with the girl, while at the same time they foreshadow what he will become.

All three are facets or variations of the same man, their world of lying pretence and complacent inertia briefly exposed both to themselves and to us by the sheer presence of the girl.

Everything is right about *Exposure*. The disciplined photography, contrasting the brightness of the landscape with the shadowy interiors of the hotel, symbolises the repressive nature of Irish life. The sparse script and Patrick Duffner's tight editing allow meaning to emerge from pauses and glances. The intimate acting and the piano music — John O'Conor and Florian Kitt playing Beethoven's variations on Mozart's *The Magic Flute* — catch the changing nuances of mood.

Not for Hickey the cosy myths so often perpetuated in literature and the visual arts of a rural Ireland that is no more and probably never was except in Paul Henry landscapes and Bord Failte brochures. *Exposure*, and its companion piece, *Criminal Conversation*, explore the tensions and evasions of a predominantly urban and industrialised Ireland in which ways of thinking lag behind the realities of everyday life.

Criminal Conversation is an up-market *Exposure*. Here is the BMW expense-account world of town houses and golf in Marbella, the promised land of the *nouveau riche* professional classes spawned by the Lemass economic miracle.

Hickey focusses on two couples who have been taken in by their own pretences. Sudden affluence has cut them off from any genuine feelings they might once have had. They are maimed without knowing it.

In *Exposure* Hickey and co-writer Philip Davison used the intrusion of a foreign girl as a catalyst to bring to the surface the repressed nature of what passes for Irish machoism, the whole chauvinist ritual of being one of the boys. This time however their device is a Christmas get-together at which a drunken game of charades tricks the characters into momentarily revealing their true selves, a shock of recognition neatly foreshadowed by the opening shot of an office party Santa losing his mask.

The rub is that both the husbands — Emmet Bergin by ostentatiously flirting with typists and the babysitter, and open-shirted Peter Caffrey with his loutish affairs on the side — basically regard their wives as the chattels the Irish constitution has traditionally made them out to be. Hence the title, which comes from the common law action upholding a husband's proprietary rights.

The wives collaborate in their own degradation, accepting a *modus vivendi* they don't really believe in because society offers them little alternative. Deirdre Donnelly busies herself with a baby, Leslie Lalor boasts about taking separate holidays and fills in time on a committee organising a Sense-of-Ireland-type touring exhibition ("We're going to have a culture-mobile to show Europe the richness of our culture"). The awful oil painting of a thatched cottage over the mantelpiece parodies her delusion. All the scenes take place in rooms, corridors, cars: the only exteriors are night-time. This heightens the sense of claustrophobia, drawing the characters in on themselves, exposing them to their own lies. Only the promiscuous baby-sitter Kate Thompson emerges as an anyway whole person: perhaps she's growing into a society in which women will finally be able to choose how to live their own lives.

1978-80

8

Black And White In Colour

Cathal Black has just finished editing his forty-two-minute feature *Our Boys* at Windmill Studios on the Dublin quays. The new studios are mainly a facility for the production of rock videos and recordings. But Black has been allowed do all his editing there without charge.

Our Boys is that kind of movie. "Peanuts isn't the word for our budget," says Black.

Much of it was shot on old black-and-white film stock scrounged from RTE. Ardmore allowed him free use of sound equipment and lighting. The Northern Ireland Arts Council put up £3,000. He started it in 1978. "But it's taken three years to get it all together."

To keep it going he's worked on other people's movies — for Bob Quinn on *Poitin* and for Joe Comerford on *Down The Corner*. "If we didn't all stick together it would be impossible to film in Ireland."

Black sets up the editing deck and runs *Our Boys* through from the beginning: its first public screening, so to speak.

Our Boys is an attempt to get to grips in an innovative and compassionate cinematic way with one of the root causes of sectarian division and social alienation in Irish life. It depicts, on both a human and an historic level, the warping effect of the so-called Catholic Irish education hammered into generations of children by the Christian Brothers.

Black intercuts a narrative account of the close-down in the early 1960s of a city school run by the Brothers with flash-back newsreel coverage of the Eucharistic Congress in 1932 in all its imperial glory. He then adds contemporary cinema verite interviews with 'old boys' who were victims of the crude 'fear of God is the beginning of wisdom' approach to education. One of the more sympathetic Brothers admits sheepishly: "This whole idea of the emotional area is very much to me a recent development."

Our Boys has the look of an intriguing preview for a full-length feature. All the ideas are introduced and a compelling treatment is suggested. There is a flow of images of cold-tiled corridors and furtive soutaned figures that tantalise the imagination and touch the raw nerve of tribal memory.

With realistic financing it has the potential to be on a par with Fred Schepsi's *The Devil's Playground*, which dealt with a similar theme in an Australian context. But Australia provided money for its film-makers throughout the 1970s: Ireland didn't. What is astonishing about *Our Boys* is that Black managed to get anything on the screen at all.

Most of the footage was shot over two years ago with the cheerful collaboration of children from Fatima Mansions. "We used an old Methodist school off the South Circular Road. It's not the sort of picture that you'd dare shoot in a Catholic school."

Black is a Christian Brother boy himself — but with a moderating touch of the Jesuits as well. "Originally I was at the CBS in Glasnevin. But I went to St Ignatius College when my family moved to Galway. Then I finished up in Colaiste Mhuire. That's where I got all the material for the picture. There's a part of me that finds it hard to forget."

Camera-man Thaddeus O'Sullivan finds it even harder to forget. Shooting *Our Boys*, Black had to keep telling him to hold back, that people wouldn't believe what they were showing, that no school could be that bad. "I still feel bitter about it," says O'Sullivan. "It fucked up a lot of people."

O'Sullivan grew up in Ranelagh in the 1950s. "We'd orchestrate our whole week around the cinemas, the Stella on weekdays, the Sandford on Friday and Saturday, the Kenilworth every Sunday night because that's where the mots went. We'd hang around McCambridge's afterwards, telling the stories of the films because that's how you judged them. It was a way of making them our own, of occupying them."

Movies were an escape from the brutalising experience of school at the Christian Brothers, Westland Row. "They were Stalinists, the way they ruled. We had a falling out from the day I got there. I was finally booted out after the Inter. It was a terrible education. We left not knowing how to learn. The awful thing was that parents went along with it. You'd come home and say, 'I got beaten up.' The answer would be, 'You must have done something, what did you do?' 'I looked round me.' I'd say. 'You looked round, well there you are.'"

First chance O'Sullivan got, he took the boat to England, working as a labourer on the Tube for three years until he qualified for a mature grant which enabled him to do graphic design for three years at Ealing College of Art, then a further three years at the Royal College of Art. "I'd become interested in photography at school, but it was like saying I was a homosexual. The reaction was, 'What on earth are you doing with a camera?'"

With grants from the English Arts Council and the BFI, he filmed *A Pint of Plain* and *On A Paving Stone Mounted,* a couple of experimental diary-type movies exploring the nature of being an immigrant in Britain. "They helped me discover that what I really love are stories.

"What you're putting on the screen is not a cheap copy of reality but a representation of reality, a kind of hyper-reality: that's what Hollywood is all about. It's a kind of realism but it's not, it's bigger than that. It's a question of not denying what the camera does to characters, to recognise that it imbues them with an emblematic quality. That you pay respect to that instead of pressing on with pseudo-reality."

The collaboration between Black and O'Sullivan on *Our Boys* is yet another instance of the support system that is developing between Irish film-makers, a further sign that while the Government dithers a *de facto* industry is developing on it own. Ten years from now it will be surprising if Ireland does not have several established directors, whatever the Government does or doesn't do.

While acting as assistant director on *Down The Corner*, Black discovered that Joe Comerford had an idea of making a film about the travelling community. He told him Neil Jordan was working on a similar synopsis of his own, and put the two in touch. After several months working together, they put together a screenplay which they entered for the 1979 £20,000 Arts Council Script Award.

"We had some settled travellers involved in filming *Down the Corner* and I got interested in their lives," says Comerford. "Ballyfermot is a community where the travellers have become well-integrated, perhaps because it's such a mixed community."

Travellers, as Comerford and Jordan have developed it, won't be so much a movie about the travelling people as a glimpse of Ireland through their eyes. "We want to show what is going on in the straight or buffer world as they see it," says Comerford.

To avoid imposing his own preconceptions on the material ("For me part of the reason for filming is to discover something first-hand about a subject"), he worked as a teacher with travellers in Ballyfermot and has spent months with them around Galway.

"You feel apprehensive at first about intruding, but there's a marvellous camaraderie about the life. It's very enjoyable sitting around a camp fire at night with a mug of tea and all the talk going on. Like being on the prairie in the Wild West.

"They love pictures, particularly Westerns. They watch them in their tents and caravans on television, which they run off the car batteries. They want me to make a Clint Eastwood type of picture. I hope they won't be disappointed."

1978-81

9

A Leap Of The Imagination

Up beyond Listowel in Kerry, the river twists and turns through wooded countryside. During a break in the 1980 Writers Week, a few of us stroll along a rough path on the river bank.

Neil Jordan is here to give a fiction workshop, Steve McDonagh to talk about Irish publishing, and Colm O Briain is here in his brief as director of the Arts Council. I'm judging a drama competition with Garry Hynes, director of the new Druid theatre company in Galway.

We come to a glade in a forest of tall trees. A rope hangs from one of the branches, dangling at the edge of a wide ditch. Children probably put it there to swing across to the other side.

While the rest of us hesitate — if you lost your grip you'd have a painful fall — Neil grabs the rope, takes a run and swings across, letting go just in time to land safely on the other side.

Neil has made a habit of taking risks and landing on his feet. Instead of playing safe after the critical success of his debut collection of short stories *Night In Tunisia*, he buried himself in the National Library and now two years later has emerged with a stunningly original first novel *The Past*. Along with Des Hogan's first novel *Leaves On Grey*, it confirms the arrival of a new generation of writers young enough to be free of the closed thinking of the De Valera era. Their reality is an Ireland of today. They have the distance to see the past objectively.

"We're the first generation that could never possibly have met Joyce and our parents could hardly have met Pearse," he says.

"So in a way, we're free of it, aren't we?"

Which is why there is irony in the title of his novel: it is not about things as they necessarily were but as they seemed to have been. A personal search for identity becomes inseparable from confusions of Irish identity. "In a way, it's paying our dues to the 'past' and to 'history'."

"Dev is first glimpsed as somebody you could have rubbed shoulders with. But by the end he has become a gaunt, dream-like schoolmaster figure shaping people's destinies. He doesn't belong to history but to myth. Yet this is the way history is remembered and this is the way it is treated. It's one of the most attractive things about growing up in Ireland, isn't it? The way the mundanity of history is transformed by unbridled imagination. That's the despair of Conor Cruise O'Brien: that you can't beat the mythologising."

The unusual structure of *The Past* is an extension of its theme. Old photographs and postcards are put before us as a mirror of earlier time through which the present becomes manifest. "People nowadays think of the past in photographs, don't they?" Jordan says.

The unorthodox shape of *The Past* gives new life to one of the most familiar themes of fiction: the discovery of self. It builds up the momentum of a psychological thriller as the series of cryptic questions posed by the narrator gradually take on flesh and blood.

The chapters come in short takes, like sequences in a movie. The pervading affinity with cinema is hardly surprising. In the two years it has taken Jordan to write *The Past* he has become increasingly involved in TV writing and film production. The camera has become an extension of his creative vision.

BBC commissioned him to dramatise *Night In Tunisia* and he has also written a treatment of his radio plays *Miracles* and *Miss Langan* which Pat O'Connor is to direct for RTE. He has scripted four episodes for RTE's major new Sean O'Casey series. "You can show all the tensions of Irish history — the tug between the

135

labour movement and the nationalist movement — through this one character," he says.

Travellers, the screenplay he wrote with Joe Comerford, won a £10,000 Arts Council Script Award. The British Film Institute then came up with an additional £45,000, a large part of their annual commitment to production.

However, differences developed with Comerford during filming. Comerford treated the finely-worked screenplay more as a working framework than as a blueprint to which reality should somehow be made to conform. The pre-ordained narrative was subordinated to the promptings of actuality Comerford found on location with the travellers. The controlled world of the writer gave way to the director's open-ended filmic responses.

Jordan was uncomfortable with this. "I think most pictures are made in the writing. The problem in most pictures is a problem of thought, not a problem of execution."

John Boorman meanwhile had seen and liked Jordan's screenplay for *Travellers*. Having long admired Jordan's short stories, he asked Jordan to collaborate with him on a screenplay for *Broken Dream*.

Frustrated with the failure of successive governments to establish a Film Board with proper financing structures, Boorman has decided instead to give a hand to anyone he thinks has potential to direct. Impressed by Jim Sheridan's *The Liberty Suit* at the Gaiety, he talked to him about doing a film script. But Sheridan instead has emigrated to the States and become involved in a theatre in New York.

Every day for three months Boorman worked with Jordan on *Broken Dream* in an office at Ardmore. A futuristic fantasy about a blind magician in a post-apocalyptic Ireland who tries to pass on his secrets to his son, they completed it in 1979. It was refused by several major studios. Boorman still hopes to get it made.

Jordan also went through the draft of *Knights* — the *Merlin* screenplay Boorman had shown me three years ago — which

Boorman has now shot as *Excalibur* on locations around Annamoe. There was talk too of an *Interview With a Vampire* project, based on a novel by Anne Rice about the destiny of a vampire in the Deep South, from the early nineteenth-century to the present day.

"I'd worked closely with John and wanted to be around during filming of *Excalibur*," says Jordan. "So we hit on the idea of me doing a documentary about it and about the Grail message that recurs in his pictures.

"It's been a very good experience for me. You're involved with lots of people. It kept me in touch with the world. You could go mad with the loneliness of just writing a novel."

It also gave Jordan the itch to direct his own screenplays. "When you write something there is always an urge to follow it right through, to put it on the screen yourself."

Charles Haughey indirectly was to make it possible for him to do so. Many commentators had written Haughey off after the Arms Trial. He'd spent the 1970s inconspicuously building up support among Fianna Fail backbenchers, playing on their feeling that the party had strayed from its republican roots. It was a tactic similar to that employed by Margaret Thatcher with disaffected Tories in the UK and it bore similarly dramatic results.

The Taoiseach Jack Lynch, who had led Fianna Fail to a record victory in 1977, rather than fight off the challenge announced on 5 December 1979 that he was resigning and that the new leader would be chosen two days later. He hoped to pre-empt Haughey and ensure the election of his close ally, George Colley. Haughey was more ready than any one had expected and won the secret ballot by forty-four votes to thirty-eight.

Two weeks before — curiously on the day my third son Jack was born: perhaps a good omen — Minister for Industry and Finance Des O'Malley had published two bills, one to regularise the National Film Studios as a semi-state company, the other to set up an Irish Film Board. With the ensuing political crisis, there were fears that it might get shelved, like the previous Bill in 1970.

The following October, however, Haughey opened the Cork Film Festival with a pledge that the Bill would be implemented. A week later it was given its second reading and it was passed in December. A Film Board was established with a revolving fund of £4.1 million. Its function would be to help get productions off the ground, whether by providing loans or underwriting grants to defray part of the overall costs, and by offering overall international marketing and distribution back-up. It was not the intention that the Board would be a major source of finance for any production: its support was seen as a way of encouraging other backers to come in.

John Boorman was appointed to the Board, along with the Industrial Credit Company's Louis Heelan and Cork Film Festival Director Robin O'Sullivan. Before the remaining four members of the Board were appointed, Boorman, Heelan and O'Sullivan, who constituted a quorum, allocated £100,000 — half its budget for the remainder of 1981 — to Neil Jordan's first screenplay *Angel*. The hurry, which outraged the Association of Independent Producers, was dictated by the fact that Channel 4, the UK's new TV channel due to come on the air the following year, had indicated its willingness to invest £400,000.

Although Boorman was executive producer — a further cause of resentment among independent film-makers who felt that having paid their dues they deserved first bite of the cherry — he stayed away from the set while Jordan was filming. "I felt my presence could only intimidate," he says. With editor Patrick Duffner — who cut all Kieran Hickey's movies — he did, however, guide Jordan in the cutting room afterwards.

Left to himself and with the experienced Chris Menges as cameraman, Jordan confounded his critics by delivering an impressively commercial thriller, rooted in the Hollywood film noir genre. The setting is Northern Ireland but the action really belongs anywhere.

Angel has intriguing affinities with Boorman's *Point Blank*, in which a gangster sets out to get his own back on a partner who has cheated him. Stephen Rea is a moody young saxophone player, familiar from American road movies, who witnesses the shooting of his band's manager — and also an innocent girl who happens to get in the way — outside a ballroom. Later he encounters one of the killers — their sectarian allegiance is deliberately ambiguous: they could be Catholic or Protestant para-militaries — and on impulse kills him with his own gun. The logic and the exhilaration of the act impel him to track down each of the other members of the gang. He becomes an avenging angel, stalking the North unsuspected even by the singer with whom he has a casual relationship.

It's a plot with metaphysical aspirations but rooted in the standard vocabulary of action cinema. Jordan has something to say about the North but the good sense not to say it. The power of violence to corrupt even the pure is implied rather than set out. Meaning is expressed not in terms of divisive polemics but in the allusive language of cinema.

This can be a fault as well as a virtue. By imposing the structures of a Hollywood genre on all too recognisable real-life situations Jordan is at times too contrived: the logic of the plot is at odds with the ambivalence of how things actually are.

Jordan captures the shabby feel of small town Ireland, the jerry-built eyesore ballroom with the flaking paint, the damp empty streets, the pervasive loneliness, a closed society turned in on itself, ruled by tribal loyalties. Not the place for an Hollywood anti-hero, which in effect is what Stephen Rea's saxophone player is. He belongs only in a movie. In the real North he'd have been knee-capped or shot long before he got near any of the killers.

Angel was to be given a special screening at the third International Festival of Film and Television in Celtic Countries in Wexford on 31 March 1982. It was like stepping into a lion's den. The Festival was a rallying point for independent film-makers. Several of them had films up for festival awards: by coincidence I was a member of the Festival jury.

The day before the screening, Tiernan McBride pinned up a notice in the foyer of the Talbot Hotel calling a meeting of all members of the Association of Independent Producers the following day at 3.45 p.m. — the same time as the screening of *Angel*. This followed a rowdy afternoon seminar at which Bob Quinn delivered a scathing attack on John Boorman. Jordan, who was present, defended Boorman and accused independent film-makers of being too "cosy".

The *Angel* screening went ahead, with over 100 delegates attending. Meanwhile at the AIP meeting, McBride read a statement denouncing Boorman's "contempt for Irish film-makers." Unknown to those present, the Cabinet was meeting in Dublin at the same time to act on new Minister for Industry and Energy Albert Reynolds' plan to close the National Film Studios. Two days later Boorman resigned as chairman of the National Film Studios and as a member of the Film Board. As a Festival jury member, I ironically found myself voting awards to Joe Comerford and Neil Jordan's *Travellers* and Bob Quinn's *Last Days of the Gaeltacht*, although our main award went to Trish Barry's 'Today Tonight' documentary *Victims of Violence.*

"I was very hurt," says Boorman, "but it passed. There was so much frustration among the independent film-makers. They'd been struggling for years to get little things done. Yet here was Neil coming through without seeming to pay his dues. Yet in fact it was Neil who really pulled it off. He went to Channel 4, Channel 4 liked it, but provided that I supervised him."

1980-82

If Boorman got over the hurt, Jordan didn't. It was to be six years before he filmed again in Ireland, and only then with the Hollywood-produced *High Spirits*. The departure of Boorman from the Film Board led to a period in which the handful of writers and directors most likely to win recognition for an Irish film industry decided to work outside Ireland. Having taking one step forward with *Angel*, Ireland's putative film industry found itself taking two steps back.

CHAPTER FIVE

HOLLYWOOD ON THE LIFFEY:

PART TWO

1

Beyond Bread And Butter

"Don't let's be parochial," says Pat O'Connor.

He's objecting to being labelled as an Irish director. "Although I don't mind it if it helps boost film-making in Ireland. But being a director is an international pursuit. Just because I'm Irish, it doesn't mean that I have to keep doing Irish pictures."

The fact that his debut feature *Cal*, like Jordan's *Angel*, is set in the North is coincidental. Helen Mirren has just won the Best Actress award at the 1984 Cannes Film Festival for her portrayal of the murdered RUC man's widow who has an affair with his IRA killer. What matters to audiences is the dilemma of lovers caught up in violence they can't control. The North merely provides a context for their tragedy.

"I would hate it to be seen as any definitive political statement on the North," O'Connor says. "The politics are right through it but only because they are part of the lives of the people."

Movies for O'Connor speak a universal language: their appeal can't be merely local. "They're a depiction of emotions. If they have a power it comes from that."

O'Connor quit RTE to direct *Cal*. Producer David Puttnam offered it to him after he won a British Academy award for the RTE/BBC co-production *The Ballroom of Romance*. "Knowing you're wanted gives you a lot of independence," he says.

Puttnam gave him a completely free hand, unusual on a first movie. "He told me everyone was there to help me make the film I wanted to make. So the flaws are all mine. I was surrounded by so much quality — people like production designer Stuart

Craig, Cameraman Jerzy Kielinski and composer Mark Knopfler — that I can have no excuses."

Not that he needs any excuses. *Cal*, true to the Bernard MacLaverty novel, is a cry from the heart of brooding intensity. Nearly everything is conveyed through the faces. "The agony is interior. I wanted to have a feeling of claustrophobia because the people are so trapped. I tried to avoid pretty pictures. We did no filming in the sunlight."

O'Connor got where he is the hard way. "You could say that I'm a late developer," he laughs.

Growing up in Waterford in the 1950s — appropriately he comes from Ardmore — he'd skip school to go to the local cinema. "You didn't have many sounding boards in rural Ireland. I learned a lot about myself through films."

Rather than go to university in Ireland — "they were so cautious then, little more than an extension of school" — he took the boat to England, where he navvied for a while, worked in a wine cellar, sold insurance and ended up a lab assistant at Oxford University.

"I saw my first Bergman films there. Where I came from, you couldn't see foreign cinema."

By nineteen he was in LA, doing film studies at UCLA, followed by a stint at film school in Toronto. "They let us loose with a Bell and Howell 16mm camera." Which got him into RTE in 1970 as a trainee, along with Ted Dolan, John Kelleher, Niall O'Briain and Joe Mulholland, cutting his teeth on documentaries. "I wasn't interested in talking heads. Reporters used despair of me. I was in agriculture, where I was pushed from Billy to Jack. People hardly knew I was there. Then Tony Barry brought me into drama."

'The Riordans' provided the crucial experience of working with actors. After two years, he graduated to single plays, notably Neil Jordan's *Miracles* and *Miss Langan*.

RTE had become the nearest thing to an Irish film industry. "It gave me a chance to learn how to make films, however badly

I did them at the time. I love that place but at the same time it's cluttered with frustrations. I wish they could give more priority to the creative elements that are there in such abundance. As a state body it has to concern itself too much with the bread and butter side. A director is regarded as troublesome it he asks for anything."

O'Connor now lives in an apartment in London's Notting Hill Gate.

BBC's Kenith Trodd, who produced *The Ballroom of Romance*, has given him a loose first draft of a screenplay by Simon Gray based on the JL Carr novel *A Month In The Country*. It's to be filmed with the Belfast-born Kenneth Branagh in the starring role. O'Connor is unlikely to return to Ireland. Yet ironically he has left RTE at a time when opportunities for creative film-making have probably never been brighter.

1984

2

Through A Broken Window

The advent of Channel 4, which under Jeremy Isaacs has committed itself to a target of twenty original films each year, has stimulated a flow of co-productions. Apart from backing *Angel*, Channel 4 has joined RTE and French TV as co-producer of the historical drama series *The Year of the French*. It also co-produced *Landings*, Brian Lynch's series dealing with German espionage in Ireland during World War, and Thomas Kilroy's version of *The Seagull*, which transfers the Chekhov play to an Irish setting.

"We've made a very conscious decision to present Ireland regularly to British audiences," says commissioning editor John Ranelagh. "We reckon that about twenty-five percent of the programmes we've got so far are either Irish-produced or have an Irish interest.

"You've got to remember that over six million people in Britain are avidly interested in Ireland for one reason or another. The readers of the *New Statesman* or *The Guardian* are interested because they're politically motivated. People who live in Kilburn or Liverpool are interested because they may be of Irish descent. Many other people are interested because Ireland is interesting. So there's a big potential there."

Channel 4 have the resources to commission the sort of off-beat documentaries RTE have been missing out on. Such as a journey by the Galway poet and politician Michael D Higgins through the West Indian island of Montserrat in search of the descendants of Irish convicts who intermarried with the African slaves brought there in the eighteenth-century and some of whom still speak with an inherited Irish accent. The most common names on the island are Ryan, Sweeney and O'Brien and St Patrick's Day is a public holiday.

Higgins, who is chairman of the Labour Party, feels the explosion of talent in the arts in Ireland of the last decade — which Channel 4 has identified and is tapping — hasn't been matched by a change in political attitudes towards culture.

To Irish politicians, art is still too often a term of derision. "It's coloured by this awful anti-urbanism, based on false nostalgia and fostered by all the official institutions," says Higgins, "the idea that if God created man in the garden, the city is the result of the fall. The real Ireland is supposed to be in the country and in the past. Yet people have been fleeing the land for generations. Conditions in traditional rural Ireland, far from being idyllic, were appalling and brutalising."

Michael D, in Dublin for a meeting of the Seanad, has called to the house in Goatstown in late autumn, 1983. Julia brings us some coffee. Just back from a disarmament conference in Prague, he's already in full flow, setting out a political vision for the arts in Irish society.

"There is no credible Socialism in the future unless it is formed by the imagination. "If you take 200,000 unemployed and add people below the poverty line and living in appalling housing, you have a definite statistical constituency for the Left. But their consciousness has to be awakened. It has been conditioned by education and religion to accept a private view of the world, the credo of private failure and private success and, when you die, private salvation. This is the bugbear. Any Socialist manifesto that doesn't address itself to the question of consciousness is doomed to failure."

Higgins maintains that Irish politics and culture are out of touch with social realities. "It's as if we're looking through a broken window. We accept a distorted view instead of getting a new glass. We live with fantasies. Democracy for most people means voting from twelve to sixteen times in their lifetime. Yet this same 'democracy' accepts that it is four times more likely for a working-class person to end up in a mental asylum and that the child of middle-class parents has eight times a better chance to receive third level education.

"Our experience of democracy excludes women from many of the key roles in life. We abuse language. We're a most undemocratic country. And yet we lecture the rest of the world on the subject.

"If Ireland is to change it will require a quantum leap of the imagination. I am not asking for a poetry of the unemployed. But I think it is reasonable to ask that there be a poetry tradition in the South that in the fullness of its experience should take in the reality of barren institutions, false language and immense social problems."

The only pity is that Higgins is in the Seanad rather than the Dail. For the time being he can fight only with words. But the challenge of politics is that it is the art of the possible. It's tempting to imagine Michael D as a Commissar for the Arts.

1982-83

3

Kiss Good-bye To History

It's certainly not Irish history as taught at school. Perhaps it's all the better for that.

Imagine filming Robert Emmet without showing his speech from the dock or even referring to it.

Not only that. Director Pat Murphy manages to leave out all the battle scenes as well.

Popular tradition casts Emmet as a romantic revolutionary with whom women fell blindly in love. But Murphy's *Anne Devlin*, premiered at Cannes Film Festival in 1984, will have none of that. Admittedly his fiancee Sarah Curran is allowed sigh a little. "But it's not a love story," insists Murphy. "There's not even a kiss." Then she laughs: "I suppose I shouldn't say that, it might put people off."

That's the whole point about the thoughtful, beautifully photographed (by Thaddeus O'Sullivan) movie she's conjured from a jail journal left by Anne Devlin, the country girl who kept house for Emmet while he was plotting his abortive rising in 1803.

"I wanted to show events entirely through her perceptions as someone who was crucial in setting everything up for the rising, but wasn't there on the day because she was a woman."

Much like her earlier movie, *Maeve*, which mirrored violence in the North from a feminist viewpoint, it deliberately challenges the male-orientated concept of politics and history.

What matters to Murphy are the little moments rather than the grandiloquent posturing. "The everyday things that have to be done and are invariably left to women to do. Things that are not normally considered worthwhile to be filmed but that are fundamental to life."

Anne, played with dignified intensity by Brid Brennan, is a Kathleen Ni Houlihaun brought down to earth, stripped of distorting myths. She impassively goes about her work while the plotters experiment like schoolboys with rockets and dress up in flamboyant uniforms that will make it easy for the British to pick them off.

"I'm saying that Emmet is important, but that all these other things are important too if we are to understand history."

Held in solitary confinement at Kilmainham Jail, under constant threat of execution, tormented by Dublin Castle's notorious interrogators, Anne Devlin holds out, refusing to inform on Emmet or on any of his accomplices.

There is a particularly telling moment, taken directly from the journal, and filmed in the same yard in Kilmainham where it actually happened, which shows Anne meeting Emmet again, shortly before his execution. "Tell them everything, Anne," he urges her, thinking she is holding out because she loves him. It doesn't occur to him that she might be keeping silent because it's the thing to do. Even he denies her intelligence.

The deliberately slow pace created by the attention to mundane detail helps evoke the sense of another age, at times almost too much so. "I had to find a way to shape the film so that it leads up to this woman in a cell confronted by her own loneliness."

Anne Devlin was financed with £230,000 put up by private investors, with the remainder of the budget coming from the Irish Film Board (£200,00), and a £60,000 Arts Council script award.

"That's the way Irish film should be financed, and I only hope it will continue."

1984

But continue it didn't. Charles Haughey pulled the plug on the Board in 1987 after it had backed ten features and about forty shorts to a total of over £2 million with virtually no return.

The trouble was that while movies like *Anne Devlin*, Cathal Black's *Pigs* and Joe Comerford's *Reefer And the Model* were well-received at festivals — Reefer even won the £150,000 Europa Prize at Barcelona — with the exception of *Angel*, and perhaps *The Country Girls*, distributors showed little interest and box-office was negligible. Without the flair, autocratic though it may have been, of Boorman, there was a distinctly parochial favour to the so-called new Irish cinema. Most of the directors who might have provided the necessary lift-off — Jordan, O'Connor, O'Sullivan — were working in the UK or Hollywood.

In place of the Board, Haughey introduced a tax shelter scheme under Section 35 of the Finance Act, 1987. Although production was to fall sharply over the next six years, the actual movies produced in this supposedly fallow period would finally serve to put Ireland on the map with world audiences.

4

One Hell Of A Weekend In Dublin

Daniel Day-Lewis is in a wheelchair, paralysed from the neck down. With a ferocious black beard he's unrecognisable from the punk homosexual in *My Beautiful Launderette* or the womanising surgeon in *The Unbearable Lightness of Being*. Even producer Noel Pearson for a moment thought he was the crippled writer Christy Brown when he came on the set of *My Left Foot*, which is on location in the Earl of Meath's mansion at Kilruddery, outside Bray, mid-summer in 1988.

The role is so physically demanding that to get into shape Day-Lewis cycled every day from Sandymount to Ardmore studios during rehearsal. He's modelled himself so much on Christy Brown that he can even dash off credible likenesses of other members of the cast with a charcoal stick between his toes. During a lunch break he has to be steered across a rutted laneway to pick up his plate of roast ham from a makeshift canteen at the rear of a lorry. To speak, he contorts his whole body, wrenching words out defiantly. "It's not a role you can turn on and off at the push of a button," says Pearson.

We're on the lawn peering in through the conservatory window. Day-Lewis can be seen getting agitated as Ruth McCabe — the nurse who later becomes his wife — tries to coax him into a reception being given in his honour by Cyril Cusack.

Director Jim Sheridan, in a blue and white striped shirt, is lining up a shot which will also take in a gathering of bow-tied extras waiting on the other side of the glass doors.

Up to now all Sheridan's work has been for the stage. But he has started well, with nearly four minutes in the can from the first day's shooting. He needed only one take for the first shot of the film, a tricky sequence in which Cusack welcomes guests arriving in their Rolls Royces.

Suddenly a walkie-talkie cackles beside us. "Can we clear the eye-lines," an assistant demands. Pearson finds some canvas chairs out of view of Day-Lewis. Nothing distracts an actor more than anyone moving in the background.

Casting Day-Lewis for the lead after his box-office success in *The Unbearable Lightness of Being* is crucial to the success of *My Left Foot*. Pearson, who bought the rights to Brown's autobiography several years ago, was able to raise nearly £1.4 million of the £1.75 million budget in London from Granada International.

When he offered the part to Day-Lewis, it had been a long shot. Pearson had never produced a movie before, Sheridan had never directed, whereas Day-Lewis was clearly a major star in the making. After his debut as a twelve-year-old delinquent in *Sunday, Bloody Sunday*, he'd gone on to win critical plaudits in *My Beautiful Launderette* and *A Room With A View* before his international breakthrough in *The Unbearable Lightness of Being*.

"Why didn't you bring it to me sooner, you bollix," he told Pearson.

"I didn't think it would be your scene," said Pearson.

"Everything is my scene," Day-Lewis replied.

It turned out he had been coming to Ireland since childhood, staying in Louisburgh with relatives of his father, Cecil Day-Lewis, who was the English Poet Laureate. He even had an Irish passport.

"What's important is not just that he's such a good actor, but that he's bankable," says Pearson. "It's the same with Ray McAnally, who plays Christy's father, and has just had such a hit with *A Very British Coup*.

Forty-six-year-old Pearson knew Christy Brown as a child. They're both from the same working class background. Pearson grew up in a family of thirteen in Crumlin. "I never really knew what I wanted to be. I thought at school I'd be a football player."

He won a minor football medal at eighteen, found work in the fruit market and became involved in trade unions. "I was a shop steward for three years, organising clerical workers into a union. It's like show business in a way. You're managing people."

He ran 'The Chessmen' showband — its guitarist was Robert Ballagh, later to become Ireland's first pop artist — in the early 1960s. He drifted into theatre almost by accident, through a meeting with Niall Toibin to discuss the possibility of getting together to make a Brendan Behan movie.

"We're still trying to get the movie together. We've finished the script and all the vibes sound good."

Pearson revolutionised Dublin theatre in 1973 with an audacious production of *Jesus Christ Superstar*. "It was the first big electrified musical. We had forty-seven mikes. There had never been anything like it here before. Pickets were outside the theatre accusing us of bringing Jesus to the gutter."

His flair is in putting entertainment packages together. Remembering Jim Sheridan from their days staging shows together at Project, he lured him back from New York with the chance of finally directing a movie.

"Coming to movies relatively late is an advantage," says thirty-nine-year-old Jim Sheridan. "It's a more affluent world than the theatre and it's very easy to live in a cocoon. Having been through the theatre, and had flops, you know that it's all just a bubble. It's a bubble that doesn't necessarily have to burst, but to stop it bursting you have to be very careful."

Sheridan grew up in the North Wall area of Dublin. "We were a big family of seven kids, and we had a lodging house. My brother died when I was seventeen and I think it fundamentally altered the family. It's hard to come to terms with a child's death and my parents' way of doing it was to go out and try and help the community. Mine was to try and get closer to my other brothers and try and protect them, because I was the oldest.

"In a funny way that led to conflict between me and my father. I was always trying to be better than him in everything. I'd have rows with him that would go on for four or five hours and all my friends used come and listen to them."

His parents started an amateur drama group called the Slot Players, performing in the local Oriel Hall — the same hall where O'Casey's first work had been staged. Sheridan made his own debut there, directing *Dr Faustus*. He went on to the Abbey School of Acting and his own children's show 'Motley' on RTE, which outraged educational authorities by attacking corporal punishment. He picked up a degree in English and Philosophy at UCD and helped launch the Project Arts Centre with Colm O'Briain and his brother Peter.

The experimental theatre staged at Project by the Sheridans in the late 1970s attracted an ensemble of new actors that included Gabriel Byrne, Liam Neeson, Olwen Fouere, Peter Caffrey and Mannix Flynn.

Project was denied its Dublin Corporation grant for hosting a visit by Gay Sweatshop in 1978, during which men kissed on the stage. Sheridan's *The Halfpenny Opera* was rubbished by critics. By then married to Fran and with two young children, Sheridan realised it was time for a move on.

"There was a sense of having to challenge yourself, and America seemed the best place to do it. Apart from our fares, we had only $40. Our apartment in New York was a small room. And there was always the worry of being illegal immigrants. It was so odd living on the edge of American society as white people."

As director of the Irish Centre on 51st Street ("a sort of Project transplanted to the States"), Sheridan provided platform for Irish writers, not always under their real names: he recently staged *The Tunnel*, a play set in the Long Kesh prison camp in the North by former inmate Terry George who had to use the pseudonym Gregory Teer.

My Left Foot is premiered at the Dublin Film Festival on 23 February 1989. By being faithful to the Brown autobiography, Sheridan has made a strength out of limitations. Rather than open out the straight-forward account of a fierce intelligence struggling to overcome the handicap of a body cruelly handicapped from birth by cerebral palsy, he closes in on it with unflinching, yet darkly comic, intensity. The range of the camera is uncompromisingly confined to that of a cripple whose left foot is the only limb over which he has any control.

By keeping the focus on the sheer physicality of being so appallingly disabled, Sheridan, working from a sharply observant screenplay written in collaboration with Shane Connaughton, plays to the hypnotic power of cinema to reveal life by seeing beneath the surface of things.

But this wouldn't be possible without the utter commitment of Daniel Day-Lewis as Brown. His performance rings true with every twitch of the shoulder and every gutteral grunt, while not for a moment slipping into caricature. Hugh O'Conor as the younger Brown has the easier task in the more heart-rending scenes, but handles himself with equal conviction.

The struggle of mind to make itself understood without the normal means of communication is a succession of little triumphs. There's the uplifting moment when the boy Christy finally manages to grip a piece of chalk between the toes and scrawl the word "mother" on the kitchen floor. "Go on Christy, make your mark," says his mother (Brenda Fricker), the only person convinced from the start that he isn't a vegetable.

By lying in the back lane, Christy develops an ability to swing his foot for penalty kicks in football matches with his pals. Blowing out the candles on his birthday cake leads to a way of breathing that enables him to begin to make intelligible sounds.

With a Dublin family proudly determined to stand up for him, he finds the confidence to take on the world on his own terms.

His alcoholic bricklayer father, a finely judged, blustering performance by Ray McAnally, even begins taking him to the local. "You're getting more like your father every day," neighbours say, reprovingly, much to Christy's delight.

There's nothing cosy about *My Left Foot*, no sentimentalising. The Christy Brown who finally surfaces is as flawed as anyone else. He doesn't conceal his hurt and anger. Nor will he be patronised. He's quite prepared to bite the hand that feeds him. "I'm glad you taught me how to speak so that I could tell you off," he tells Fiona Shaw as Eileen Cole, the therapist who encourages him to paint and write. He's always awkward to be with. "You're not afraid of me, you're afraid of yourself," he tells Ruth McCabe, the nurse who eventually marries him.

Laced with irreverent Dublin wit, *My Left Foot* is a memorably human entertainment with universal appeal, rooted as it is in the theme of triumph over impossible odds — the most enduring of all movie genres.

Pearson plays a hunch and decides to go with the largely untried new independent distributors Miramax for *My Left Foot*'s American release at the end of 1989. They release it selectively in just two cinemas at the end of November to build up critical word-of mouth and qualify for the Oscars. It pays off. Day-Lewis picks up most of the major acting awards in the run-up to Oscar nominations. Miramax take over the Hearing Room of the Hart Senate Building in Washington DC on 7 February 1990 for a special showing for the disabled. Edward Kennedy, Bob Dole and other politicians mix with moguls and stars. Television cameras are everywhere. Day-Lewis, only months after his breakdown on the stage of the National Theatre in London while playing Hamlet, says that he's only doing the publicity rounds for the sake of the disabled and sufferers from cerebral palsy.

When the Oscar nominations are announced the next week, *My Left Foot* is up for best picture, best director, best adapted screenplay, best supporting actress and best actor, an astonishing achievement by a low-budget $2 million movie by an unknown director. Miramax widen the release of *My Left Foot* and its grosses soar from $2.8 million to $14.4 million by the night of the Oscar Awards.

Against the odds, Day-Lewis beats off the challenge of Tom Cruise in *Born On the Fourth of July*, Morgan Freeman in *Driving Miss Daisy*, Robin Williams in *Dead Poets Society* and fellow Irishman Kenneth Branagh in *Henry V*. Brenda Fricker also wins Best Supporting Actress, and Sheridan and Connaughton win the adapted screenplay Oscar. Accepting his award, Day-Lewis promises "one hell of a weekend in Dublin." It's a phrase that encapsulates *My Left Foot*'s achievement and catchingly heralds Ireland's arrival as a movie force.

1987-89

5

The Niggers Of Dublin

Dublin teacher Roddy Doyle has a couple of things to get out of the way before he goes back to school after the summer holidays in 1990.

Around the corner from Greendale in Kilbarrack where Doyle teaches Geography and English, Alan Parker is starting to shoot the film version of *The Commitments*, Doyle's first novel about a group of North city youths — "the niggers of Dublin" — who try to form a soul band inspired by the black music of James Brown.

"I'd just like to look in on the shoot for a couple of days," he says. "I've never been on a set before. I'm curious to see how it's done."

The Commitments was originally published by King Farouk, a one-off publishing imprint specially set up by Doyle's pals at the Passion Machine — the innovative theatre group operating out of community halls that produced his plays *Brownbread* and *War*. It sold out within weeks, was picked up by Heinemann and Picador and acclaimed in the US by *The Village Voice* and *The New York Times*, which likened it to "a veritable Berlitz course in the city's colourful, sexual street slang." It's the way people speak rather than what they say that matters to Doyle. Not just any people, but Northsiders. "Don't expect any messages about the world, politics or the dole," he says. "As far as I'm concerned, the message is the characters."

For *The Commitments* he had to experiment with ways of spelling Northside colloquialisms he'd pick up from his pupils.

"I'd try them out in the bath." Some Dublin literary critics were aghast at the outspoken language. "They claimed to object to it on aesthetic grounds. But you might just as well object to life on aesthetic grounds. I make no apologies. It's the way kids talk. But not in class, of course."

For Parker, operating out of Jury's Hotel, *The Commitments* harks back to his own youth in North London after the war. "It may be particular to Dublin. I don't think anyone will understand a word of the language. But the experience is true to young people everywhere in the world who have ever tried to put a band together."

He's proved right when *The Commitments* opens in Los Angeles the following summer. A glossary is issued before the premiere, just to make sure the celebrity audience appreciate the nuances of poxy, tosser, gobshite, bollix, bleedin', pisser, wanker and shag off.

It isn't needed. Defying all predictions that a Dublin soul musical starring complete unknowns wouldn't travel, *The Commitments* becomes a surprise summer hit. "20th Century Fox have a genuine sleeper on its hands, a music-crammed film whose appeal could extend from contemporary college kids all the way up to those with fond memory for the soul hits of the 1960s," predicts the *Hollywood Reporter*. The teenage magazine *Seventeen* enthuses: "One of the funniest, most original flicks we've seen in ages."

Mordantly comic in its defiance of the graffiti-scarred, concrete-block bleakness of its Darndale settings, *The Commitments* could have been scripted by a Beckett high on Otis Redding. Its absurdist humour is typified by a shot of a youth waiting with a horse for a lift in the piss-drenched hallway of a block of flats. "You're not taking the horse in the lift, are you?" "Yeah, sure the stairs would kill him."

What matters most of all is that it's the first movie accurately — even angrily, yet lovingly too — to reflect the actual living reality of urban Ireland and the urban Irish, warts and all. It's a breakthrough movie, daringly but triumphantly showing that a universal audience can be reached by being honest to a particular Irish experience.

Alan Parker has watered down none of Doyle's often scurrilous Dublinese. He has coaxed and coached his cast of youngsters — filtered from thousands of auditions — into an ensemble of performers who, both as actors and musicians, gell together with a wit and fluency that makes them compulsively watchable (and, just as important, listenable).

Although it's non-stop music — fifty-two songs and sixty-eight musical cues evoking the throbbing range of 1960s soul — *The Commitments* is not in fact a musical. The characters and their relationships, their homes and haunts, the harsh documentary look of a Dublin of the dispossessed sweep you along. They fuel the music and are fuelled by it, catching in their voices the voice of youth everywhere, jobless and marginalised in rundown estates and tower blocks, dreaming of being anywhere except where they are.

Doyle didn't attend the LA premiere. He had a reading to give in Manchester. He wouldn't have gone anyway. "It's a long way to go to see a movie," he says. "I'd have had nightmares of trying to make small talk with celebrities like Kevin Costner. All that hype, with people patting me on the back all the time, would be too much for me." He found the whole business of filming very bureaucratic. "Only the end result is good. If it hadn't been, I would have found it an embittering experience."

So much so that he's insisting on retaining control of the filming of *The Snapper*, a follow-up to *The Commitments* also set in the same imaginary North Dublin housing estate of Barrytown and again featuring the Rabbite family. It turns upside down all the pious cliches about unmarried mothers. "Getting pregnant without being married isn't a huge big moral scandal any more. It's not like the fifties when you sneaked off to England. Attitudes have changed."

He's written the screenplay himself and it will be directed by Stephen Frears. There are also plans to film *The Van*, which completes his Barrytown trilogy.

Barrytown is loosely based on the Darndale estate, adjoining Kilbarrack, where Doyle was born in 1958. His father, who worked in the manpower training agency Anco, had a penchant for playing the banjo, which probably provided the early genesis for *The Commitments*.

After a Christian Brothers education, Doyle qualified as a teacher, joining the staff of Greendale Community School in 1980. Although his novels and plays have by now made him financially independent, he has no intention of giving up teaching. "I'll stick to it for inspiration and because I like it."

He lives in Killester with his publicist wife Belinda Moller and their six-month-old baby Rory, availing of school holidays to do most of his writing. "Three months off is terrific. No attendance figures to worry about. It clears your head completely. But I won't mind going back."

1989-91

6

Interview With A Director

"Once you've done a big movie, you're not supposed to go back," says Neil Jordan. "Eventually you end up just doing Hollywood movies. You get lost in being a journeyman director."

Yet after the $30 million Paramount blockbuster *We're No Angels*, starring Robert De Niro, Sean Penn and Demi Moore, here's Jordan back in Ireland in 1990, shooting the tiny £2.5 million *The Miracle*.

It's an idea that wouldn't go away — and didn't belong in Hollywood — about a youth who falls in love with a woman who turns out to be the mother he thought was dead.

"So I wrote it over Christmas, upstairs in my home here in Bray where all the action would take place," he says.

Stephen Woolley, who set up Palace Pictures in 1983 to produce Jordan's second movie *The Company of Wolves*, put the finance together even before the screenplay was written. "Which has made it all happen very quickly. I was relieved it was so small. It allows for great simplicity."

Jordan wrote *The Miracle* for Donal McCann and for Beverly D'Angelo, the American actress with whom he became involved during the filming of *High Spirits* and who now shares his Victorian terraced house at the end of the esplanade in Bray. James Joyce lived for a while as a child in the house next door, which is the setting for the Christmas dinner row scene over Parnell in *Portrait of the Artist*.

The Miracle is being shot almost entirely on their doorstep. "I get up each morning, walk to the door, go into the house two doors down which has exactly the same structure as this house and which we've redone as a set, shoot the movie, go down the promenade and do a little more, then come back and go asleep. Day after day."

When Donal McCann, who plays the father, has a dream, it's a dream Jordan actually had. "For once in my life as a director I can say to the entire unit, that's not the way it was, I dreamed this, the man was standing exactly there."

Filming has become almost like a waking dream, at times too much so. "I walk out the door and the set is there. If you did that too often you'd develop extreme problems of perception, of what is real and what isn't."

Perhaps that's why he's sold the house to singer Mary Coughlan, whom he launched as an actress in *High Spirits*. But he'll still be living within sight of Bray Head. He's bought a £400,000 house on Sorrento Terrace in Dalkey, overlooking Killiney Bay.

The Miracle has developed into a probing of the confusion between dream and reality. Niall Byrne and Lorraine Pilkington, two unknowns Jordan has cast as the boy and his girl-friend, play games imagining stories for strangers they encounter walking along the promenade.

Much as Jordan himself did, fantasizing about becoming a writer, when he'd come to Bray for summer holidays with his mother's family. "My memory of that age is generally of using words I didn't understand. You thought you knew things you didn't."

Nothing is quite real in *The Miracle*: even Bray is transformed into something else, a magical landscape where elephants and lions romp on the esplanade. "It's a kind of paradox about filming. You have to alter what is there to make it true."

Jordan promised Woolley "a very small picture." But despite its small budget, it is turning out be hugely complex. It isn't just a matter of rehearsing an entire band and virtually creating a circus on the lawn in Martello Terrace, bringing in speciality acrobatic acts from the continent to augment Fossetts Circus. For the play within a film, *Destry Rides Again*, in which D'Angelo appears, he has had to stage a musical in the Gaiety, directed by Patick Mason, complete with chorus and four big numbers. "But stuff like that is great to do. The difficult things in filming are the small little scenes where true emotions are being expressed."

Jordan relishes working again on a small scale. Unlike *High Spirits* ("a dreadful, heart-breaking experience. It took two years out of my life. It's the only thing I've ever done which I've not been able to finish"), the size of the budget isn't dictating what he can do. "The trouble with Hollywood is that you get tremendously well paid and get used to that system of making movies. But you've got that thing called a soul, haven't you, to look after as well."

After the *Angel* row in 1982, Jordan made *The Company of Wolves* and *Mona Lisa* in the UK with Woolley. He became established as a "British" director. When he won a Golden Globe for *Mona Lisa* it was acclaimed as a "British" triumph. But he has never considered himself as anything other than an Irish director. "There's a tendency here not to regard you as Irish if you don't make movies set in Ireland and concerned with problems of Irish identity. Yet I see everything I do as dreadfully Irish in so many ways."

The Crying Game, his next project, could hardly be more overtly Irish. He's written it for Stephen Rea, the saxophone player in his debut film *Angel*, who this time is cast as a Provo gunman who kidnaps a black British soldier in South Armagh.

By giving him a conscience Jordan daringly undermines the preconceptions that make the seemingly endless chain of atrocities in the North so incomprehensible. Confronted by a human being rather than a stereotype Brit — when through curiosity he allows his captive to take off his hood — Rea becomes prey to the human feelings he has been trained to suppress, and he too ceases to be a stereotype. From that moment he is both lost and saved, alienated from his own world but unlikely to find a place in any other.

It's a depressing comment on the state of the Irish film industry that *The Crying Game* is proving difficult to finance, despite its modest $4 million budget. Shooting is delayed several months in 1991 as Jordan struggles to find backers.

"First of all it's about an uncomfortable issue Irish people don't like to look at very much," he says. "Then you've got the racial thing, which probably put the Americans off, and the sexual thing, and all the blood and guts. I sent it to people I know in LA, who thought it was wonderful, but they didn't think anyone in the world would take a chance on it. Eventually we've had to do it without any American financing, which is good, because they would have interfered. They probably would have killed it."

Rescue came through Nippon finance. Japanese backing has now become a major factor in financing independent film-making, perhaps because the Japanese don't believe in interfering. "They kind of follow individuals."

The Crying Game, premiered out of competition at the 1992 Venice Film Festival, gloriously defies classification. To say that it's three-movies-in-one might suggest a disjointed, episodic structure, which isn't the case. The function of Jordan's screenplay is to deconstruct popular assumptions not only about the North but about racism and sexuality. *The Crying Game* achieves this, much like Hitchcock's *Psycho*, through two sudden and shocking switches in direction. It starts out seeming to be a movie about political confrontation. A relationship seems likely to develop between Rea and his black hostage, Forrest Whitaker, building up to some tragic or uplifting denouement. But the denouement comes a mere third of the way through the movie. Suddenly we're plunged into a totally different set up. Rea is in London, working on a building site and looking for a girl whose photograph haunts him. When he finds her, conventional romantic expectations are triggered. Played by newcomer Jaye Davidson, she's a black girl with long crimped hair and the most beautiful face.

We're as captivated with her as Rea is, and we settle in to this second movie. But then again, it all falls apart in one of the most startling nude love scenes ever filmed. The girl, like everyone else, is not what she seemed. As before with his hostage, Rea is forced to accept someone in their own right rather than impose his own idea on her of what she should be.

The Crying Game's moral is delivered with violent force as Jordan shifts into yet another gear. We're now drawn into a thriller of retribution and revenge, with the girl innocently caught in the middle as Rea's past and hers catch up on them.

Although *The Crying Game* explores the most complex emotions, and keeps changing mood and pace, it is told by Jordan with classic simplicity, and without tricks. It weaves between different movie forms, subverting everything that audiences take for granted, opening eyes. "That's what I used like in movies, the way they could change your idea of the world," he says. "Cinema should illuminate the soul in some way."

Hollywood mightn't have been prepared to back *The Crying Game* but, prompted by a shrewd Miramax release which plays on the ingenious surprise sex twist, it now showers it with six Academy Award nominations — and this in the year of Clint Eastwood and *Unforgiven*.

Jordan comes home to Killiney with the best screenplay Oscar and the knowledge that *The Crying Game*'s US gross of $60 million plus — on a budget of $4 million — makes it one of the most lucrative 'British' movies ever. His new bankability raises hopes for his long delayed plan to film Michael Collins.

"I'm not someone who spends their entire life trying to make a film about Collins," he says. "It just irritates me that it's there and I haven't been able to film it. I've got this script that's like *The Godfather* to the power of seven. But to get Hollywood to commit $30 million for a film about a bunch of desperadoes who tore apart the British empire and invented the technique of terrorism as we know it, well, it hasn't been a very good pitch."

1990-92

7

A Traveller's Tale

Gabriel Byrne in Mike Newell's *Into the West*, premiered in October 1992, plays a widowed traveller who has quit the road for a high-rise flat in Ballymun. "We're all travellers in one way or another," he says at one point, "but we're never sure where we're going."

He might just as well have been talking about himself. His see-saw career as would-be priest, archaeologist, language teacher and RTE soap star has taken him from Walkinstown to Hollywood and back — with a marriage to Ellen Barkin along the way. "But I couldn't stay here. I have now such an advanced stage of wanderlust that I find I have to keep moving on."

Going to the pictures at the Apollo and the Star in Crumlin in the 1950s and daydreaming of the Wild West — like the two little boys who run away in *Into the West* — was the start of it. But when he did leave Dublin at the age of twelve, he didn't get beyond Birmingham, where he spent four years in a seminary. "The priests knew what they were doing," he says. "It was extremely alluring to a kid. Everything was marvellously strange. The smell of the air, the names of the shops — like Uriah Crump, undertaker — the policemen's helmets. Birmingham was particularly exotic, because I'd never seen a black person before."

After training as an archaeologist at UCD, he was off again, this time to Spain, where he taught English in Bilbao. "I was about thirty-five years too late for the Spanish Civil War, but that's actually what I was going for. That Hemingway-esque

George Orwell type of adventure you always thought would happen to you there. It never really panned out. Bilbao was a filthy industrial city. I was working in a shady set-up, where I had to cross the border every three months to change passports. Most of the people there had left Ireland under some kind of cloud."

Back in Ireland again, working as a teacher, he began helping his pupils stage plays. The father of one of them, who was member of the Abbey Theatre, told him, 'You should do this for a living.' So he did, first in the Abbey and then the Royal Court in London.

Within a couple of years John Boorman cast him in *Excalibur*. Soon afterwards he was a regular in RTE's 'The Riordans' and later 'Bracken'. "It was a tremendous learning experience. Not just for me but for directors like Pat O'Connor. Shooting for three days, rehearsing for a week. It was really great grounding for working with cameras."

In the 1980s his dark brooding presence made him a leading international star — particularly impressive in *Defense of the Realm* and the Coen Brothers' *Miller's Crossing* — yet he has never lost touch with Ireland. "Now that I'm moving into production, the kind of films I want to produce are movies that come from here. I'm not interested in producing Hollywood blockbusters. I want to produce movies about here that I feel passionate about."

He helped raise the money for *Into the West*, Jim Sheridan's first screenplay, written before *My Left Foot*, which highlights the marginalisation of travelling people in Ireland.

Sheridan has now teamed up again with Daniel Day-Lewis to direct a Byrne project — *In the Name of the Father*, based on the Guildford Four scandal. "It's not just about a horrendous miscarriage of justice. It examines the whole notion of how we perceive justice and also the whole Irish and English experience in that to be Irish in England is to be automatically guilty, like a black in America."

With Irish actors nominated three years in a row for Oscars — Daniel Day-Lewis, Richard Harris for Sheridan's *The Field* in 1991 and this year Stephen Rea in *The Crying Game* — Byrne is suddenly no longer a novelty in Hollywood. Leading men are increasingly talking with an Irish accent.

Patrick Bergin, a brother of *Criminal Conversation* star Emmet Bergin, made his breakthrough in Bob Rafelson's *Mountains of the Moon* and is now co-starring with Julia Roberts in *Sleeping with the Enemy*.

One-time Project regular Liam Neeson is Diane Keaton's husband in *The Good Mother* and a high-tech human monster in Sam Raimi's chiller *Darkman*.

Even Pierce Brosnan has made up for the awful *Taffin* by starring in Bruce Beresford's *Mister Johnson*, William's Boyd's adaptation of the Joyce Cary novel.

And moving up fast is thirty-three-year-old Aidan Quinn, first seen in *Desperately Seeking Susan*, and now starring in Barry Levinson's *Avalon*. Although Chicago-born, Quinn spent most summers as a child back in the Ireland his parents had left. That's how he first got the idea that maybe he could become an actor. "When I was eighteen I lived for a while on the Northside, skivvying in some godawful restaurant, trying to make ends meet delivering posters and selling *In Dublin*, whatever it took."

He'd go to the Trinity Players lunchtime shows, "as much for the soup and sandwiches as anything else." Project too, where he got to know Jim and Peter Sheridan. "When I saw Peter's *The Liberty Suit*, I remember thinking, I want to do that. But being a stranger, American and yet Irish, I didn't really have the guts to make a go of it."

Back in Chicago, Quinn got work as a roofer on construction sites. "But I didn't want to end up like the guys I was working with. They were great guys but they were all alcoholics. They'd think nothing of emptying a whisky bottle at seven in the morning."

With his rugged Mel Gibson looks, he was cast in a lead role by his drama teacher almost as soon as he started classes. "All of a sudden people were introducing me as an actor, which was ludicrous. But it sure beat roofing."

While appearing off Broadway in Sam Shepard's *Fool for Love* and *A Lie Of The Mind*, he met up again with Jim Sheridan. "Jim is a tough little bastard. He's great. I love him. I'd be doing a play and he's come by afterwards. He'd show me a script. 'What do you think of this,' he'd say, 'how am I going to get the money for this.' I'd read the script and it would be brilliant. I'd make some calls. But it was always the same. I'd end up saying, 'I wish I could help you, Jim, but I don't have the clout. But it's going to happen one day.'"

1992

And so it has. Not just for Quinn and for Sheridan. But for the Irish film industry. And the unlikely trump card that is finally to launch Ireland into the movie mainstream is put on the table as the result of a freak Irish political deal.

CHAPTER SIX

ARDMORE: THE SEQUEL

The telephones of journalists Geraldine Kennedy and Bruce Arnold were tapped by the Gardai on the instructions of Fianna Fail Justice Minister Sean Doherty in 1982. When this was revealed in the Dail by Michael Noonan, the Fine Gael Justice Minister who succeeded him, Fianna Fail leader Charles Haughey accepted general responsibility, but denied any knowledge of the tapping. Doherty was obliged to resign from the Fianna Fail front bench.

A Phone Tapping Bill, published by the Fianna Fail/Progessive Democrat government, unexpectedly revived the affair in December 1991. Doherty, now Cathaoirleach of the Seanad, regarded it as a personal affront. He issued a statement claiming that Haughey had been fully aware that the phones were being tapped.

Haughey's supporters were convinced that Doherty was put up to it by aspiring Taoiseach Albert Reynolds and Padraic Flynn, whom Haughey contemptuously dubbed the "Country and Western" alliance.

Haughey gave a press conference at which he rejected Doherty's claim as totally false. The Progessive Democrats, however, implied that they might withdraw from government if Haughey didn't step down. On 30 January 1992 he amazed everyone by doing just that. Albert Reynolds was promptly chosen as his successor.

In the following months Reynolds could scarcely contain his eagerness to prove himself with the voters. He thought he saw his chance in the run up to Christmas and called a snap General Election. It turned out to be an appalling gaffe. The Fianna Fail vote dropped disastrously, leaving them with a mere sixty-eight seats to Fine Gael's forty-five and Labour's highest ever thirty-three.

The normal logic of Irish politics pointed to another Fine Gael/Labour coalition. Instead Labour responded to the new mood in politics reflected by their triumph at the polls — and by their candidate Mary Robinson's win in the Presidential Election — by forging a deal with Fianna Fail.

When all the balances in the Coalition partnership were put in place, it turned out that a poet, Labour's Michael D Higgins, had control of a new Department of Arts, Culture and the Gaeltacht. The importance attached to the new Department was indicated by the fact that Higgins was to be a full member of the Cabinet.

One of the first decisions made by Higgins was to appoint former Arts Council director Colm O'Briain as his special adviser.

At the opening of Dublin Film Festival the following month, programme director Martin Mahon suggested that the lack of an Irish film to open the festival had to do with the Government's failure to support a film industry. Higgins promptly stepped up and promised to put things right. He formally announced a White Paper, to report by the end of the year. He talked of some form of revamped Film Board. He talked of direct State subvention. He gave an assurance that by 1996 an Irish film industry would be up and running.

It turned out that he was being too modest.

Within a year the Irish Film Board had been resurrected — chaired by Lelia Doolan — with a £10 million budget for development and production over five years. Legislation was introduced requiring RTE to spend twenty percent of its programme budget on independent productions by 1999. The scope of Section 35 of the 1987 Finance was greatly widened, providing generous tax breaks for film investment. Ireland joined Eurimages. And Higgins announced the establishment of a third national television service for Irish language broadcasting, Teilifis na Gaeilge, which would involve the commissioning of approximately 700 hours of programmes from the independent sector.

By 1994, £50 million had been attracted into film production under Section 35, and a further £40 million approved. When Higgins heard that Mel Gibson was having second thoughts about shooting his $53 million Highlands epic *Braveheart* in Scotland, he contacted him personally, filled him in on Section 35, offered him the Irish Army as extras and persuaded him to relocate most of the production at Ardmore Studios.

With Disney Television's *Old Curiosity Shop* just about to wrap and a full slate of productions lined up for the rest of the year, Ardmore was running at full capacity for the first time since being established in 1958. Closed down by Albert Reynolds in 1982, the studios for a while became a base for Mary Tyler Moore's TV series. They were subsequently taken over by the UK independent Television South, before being acquired in 1990 by the rock band U2's manager, Paul McGuinness.

"Unless there's a flow of production activity, we're dead in the water," says chief executive Kevin Moriarty. "The mistake in the past was to think the studios alone could be an industry. They can't. They're just one element in the infrastructure. You can't maintain studios if there are just one-off productions here and there."

Until 1993 Ireland averaged about two films a year. Up to thirty were scheduled to shoot in 1995. It has got so that Ireland is running out of crews to man them. Columbia TriStar's *Sense And Sensibility* and United Artists' *Richard I*, cancelled their plans to shoot in Ireland and relocated in the UK. Neil Jordan had to import people from the UK for Warner's $27 million *Michael Collins*, with Liam Neeson in the title role, which he started shooting in and around Dublin in July, 1995.

Coming soon after *The Crying Game*, the success of *Interview With a Vampire* — which topped $100 million in the US — finally won Jordan the clout to bring *Collins* to the screen. David Geffen, one of Hollywood's most powerful moguls, who is in the process of forming a $2 billion studio with former Disney boss Jeffrey Katzenberg and Steven Spielberg, and who gave Jordan final cut on *Vampire*, is again backing him.

If there was to be a price for Jordan's rise to the status of a major Hollywood player, it seemed it might be the curtailment of his literary career. Yet coinciding with the release of *Vampire*, he published *Sunrise With Sea Monster*, his first novel in over ten years. "I didn't even know I'd write another book," he says. "Every year I'd say I was going to do it, but then I'd do another film. I'd written it out in my head, so finally I took the phone off the hook for four months and wrote it."

Sunrise With Sea Monster, set during the Spanish Civil War and in Ireland amid the lunatic politics of the wartime Emergency, confronts the dilemma of a man forced to betray everything that matters to him. At its core is the strange erotic relationship between a father, his son and the young music teacher who comes into their lives in their terraced house in Bray. Distinctions between the real and the imagined blur in a magical tour-de-force, triggered by memories of a past that is still present.

One of the most vivid of these is of a boy playing with his father's loaded gun. "I put one bullet in the chamber, spun it, then stuck the barrel in my ear and listened to the sound of the trigger as I pulled."

It might be a metaphor for Jordan's daring in the high risk world of international film production.

Jordan still has hopes of getting together again with John Boorman to realise the *Broken Dream* project that originally brought them together. "We never seemed to get it right," says Boorman, whose *Beyond Rangoon* was premiered at the 1995 Cannes Film Festival. "But I read it recently and it's absolutely marvellous. It didn't seem to connect before but now the world seems to have grown into it. It seems exactly right for now."

Boorman still lives in Annamoe, although he has separated from Christel. When he's not filming, he plants trees. "It's become a big part of my life. This is a tree planet, but we've mostly got rid of the trees. Without trees, the planet cannot survive."

In one winter alone he put down 13,000 native broad leaf oak trees. His valley is growing back to the forest it once was. "Fortunately up around here there are fragments of primeval oaks forest that are almost unmatched anywhere in Europe. They've just been left, largely through neglect. There's a lot to be said for benign neglect."

Ironically, Irish film-makers too made their initial international breakthrough during a period of benign neglect after the closedown of the Film Board and the collapse of Ardmore. Cinema is supposedly the ultimate collaborative art but its achievements are invariably the result of individual brilliance and persistence.

The huge individual box-office successes of *My Left Foot*, *The Commitments* and *The Crying Game* established Ireland's reputation in Hollywood as a bankable co-production partner and an economically attractive location for filming.

Pat O'Connor, having made his name as a director by filming abroad, has now, like Jordan, been lured back to Ireland. He's bought a second home in Cork where he'll live part of each year with his American actress wife Mary Elizabeth Mastrantonio, whom he met while filming his comedy thriller *The January Man*.

He too has shown daring. His seemingly parochial $9 million adaptation *Circle of Friends*, a Maeve Binchy novel about three Irish country girls who come to university in the city, has struck an unexpected chord in the States, staying in the Top Twenty box-office chart for fifteen weeks.

It encapsulates a late 1950s Irish spirit of innocent defiance. "I've tried to make it a little bit of a laugh here and there, which isn't that hard coming from that background myself," he says. It works because although it's true to an Ireland that survives only in nostalgia, its theme is universal. "Kids everywhere pretend to know more than they do," says O'Connor. "We're all a timorous species under the surface, whatever our age."

Jim Sheridan has taken a break from filming to reunite with his brother Peter and one-time Project collaborator in a new staging of James Plunkett's *The Risen People*. Peter appeared as a priest in Sheridan's *In the Name of the Father*, which broke all Irish box-office records. Sheridan's mother and father also had parts: it finished up something of a home movie. Based on Gerry Conlon's account of his experiences as one of the Guildford Four, thrown into prison with his father Guiseppe for an IRA bombing neither of them knew anything about, it gave Sheridan a chance to lay some of the ghosts of his own relationship with his father.

"When you get to be forty, you begin to understand your father more. Because it's difficult to talk to your father when you're young. You have this father and son in a cell together and they have to talk. And in a way it was me coming to terms with my own father."

Noel Pearson has teamed up with an English director, Michael Lindsay-Hogg, to produce *Frankie Starlight*, a dwarf's view of the romance which brought his French mother to Ireland after the War. It's based on a novel by Chet Raymo which was sent to Pearson by a friend, Fr Bartly McFadden. "The cover was very Oirish, complete with leprechauns and shamrocks," says Pearson. "It lay on my desk for several weeks." Then he flipped it open and saw a note: "This could be your Right Foot."

Section 35 is showing spectacular results. But the boom in filming, which has turned Ireland into a vast movie lot, isn't simply the result of financial factors and shrewd Government support. Movies are proving to be a natural outlet for Ireland's rich talent in writing.

Jordan's strength as a director comes from his writing. So much so that he told David Geffen that he would only direct *Interview with A Vampire* if he could do his own draft of the screenplay. "I said to him I won't be able to do this unless I have the freedom."

Geffen replied: "I'll make sure you have freedom."

My Left Foot was written by Sheridan in collaboration with author Shane Connaughton, who has since scripted the autobiographical *The Playboys* (starring Aidan Quinn) and *The Run of the Country*, both filmed on location in Redhills, Co Cavan, the Border village where he grew up. He likens the experience to "getting another crack at my childhood."

Playwright Hugh Leonard has immortalised his Dalkey childhood in a succession of movies. He even made a Hitchcock-like appearance in the film version of his Tony Award-winning Broadway hit *Da*, playing one of the pallbearers at his father's funeral. He can be heard ad-libbing the commentary as the pilot of a river tour-boat in *Widow's Peak*, which he wrote for Mia Farrow. They're now planning a follow-up comedy murder thriller *Bandjaxed*. "I love being here," says Mia Farrow, whose mother Maureen O'Sullivan — she played Jane to Johnny Weismuller's Tarzan — came from Boyle, Co Roscommon. "It'll be easy to come back. I think of living here."

Novelist, playwright, and publisher Dermot Bolger, an inspirational figure in the emergence of a new generation of Irish writers like Eoin McNamee and Ferdia MacAnna (whose novel *Last of the High Kings* is being filmed by Gabriel Byrne), is increasingly turning to movies. His screenplay based on Carl Lombard's *The Disappearance of Finbar* has finished shooting on location in Lapland and Tallaght. Lynda Myles, who produced *The Commitments*, has also taken an option on his novel *A Second Life*.

Joe O'Connor, who won the 'Hennessy New Writer of the Year Award' in 1989, has teamed up with director Padraic Breathnach to follow up their short features *A Stone Of the Heart* and *The Long Way Home* with a German/French/Irish co-production *Ailsa*, which won a £250,000 production prize at San Sebastian Film Festival. "It's the first time we've actually made a film where we're actually paying people," says producer Ed Guiney.

Joe Comerford continues to go his stubbornly independent way. He produced *High Boot Benny* on a tiny £500,000 budget. Shot on Super 16mm and blown up to 35mm and set on the border, it's a strange and darkly disturbing look at attempts by a liberal-minded Protestant woman and an ex-priest to keep their school for delinquent children free from the conflict around them. *High Boot Benny* is an allegory, seen through the wounded but trusting eyes of a youth who has found a home there, about the impossibility of ordinary people staying neutral amid the violence and religious bigotry that divides Ireland. It's the sort of deeply personal and uncompromisingly probing film unlikely to garner Oscar nominations or register strong in the box-office charts. Its appeal is unapologetically to a minority art-house audience.

"The basic reason I make films is to make art," says Comerford. Having battled as an independent film-maker for twenty-five years, during which he has produced ten movies, he should be feeling more optimistic now that a properly funded Irish Film Board has been resurrected — but typically he's not. "The Film Board is under tremendous pressure to be profitable. There is a very large grouping within the film industry which does not really want film as an art form. We've arrived at the stage in Ireland where some people will chose to make movies, and other people will chose to make films. What I'm asking for is co-existence. If there isn't an acknowledgement of the diversity of film-making and the importance of film as an art form, I'm not going to survive."

Comerford's friend and frequent collaborator Cathal Black isn't just surviving: with *Korea*, which closed the 1995 Dublin Film Festival, he has created an hauntingly elegiac meditation on the culture of violence passed from fathers to sons in Ireland. It's love story adapted from a work by John McGahern — the second time they have collaborated — which revolves around the return home for burial of a young Irish emigrant killed in the Korean War. In its quiet, thoughtful and compassionately performed manner, it's one of the most beautiful movies yet produced in Ireland, comparable in its sense of landscape to Thaddeus O'Sullivan's debut feature *The December Bride*.

O'Sullivan quickly followed up *The December Bride* with *Nothing Personal* for Channel 4, a thriller about Protestant loyalist paramilitaries in the North during the 1975 IRA ceasefire. During pre-production the IRA called their August 1994 ceasefire which signalled a possible end to the North's twenty-five years of bloodshed and murder, giving it an eerie frisson.

Nothing Personal, which was premiered at Galway Film Fleadh, has become the first Irish movie to make the official selection for the Venice Film Festival. O'Sullivan is now working with John Banville on a screenplay based on his award-winning novel *The Book of Evidence*. "It's a very challenging book in terms of how the story is told," says O'Sullivan. "Finding a film equivalent for that is a challenge we're both enjoying."

Sadly the Film Board came too late for Kieran Hickey. Unable to continue filming in the Republic in the 1980s, he moved his operations to the North, filming his John McGahern adaptation *The Rockingham Shoot* for the BBC, with Danny Boyle producing. One of the first projects backed by the revamped Film Board was a Hickey screenplay, but he died in 1993 while it was still in pre-production.

Michael D Higgins didn't create the Irish film industry. But without him it might never have taken off. The people and conditions needed to bring it about had gradually and often unnoticed come together both in Ireland and abroad. By a political accident, Higgins was the right man in the right place at the right time. He had the flair and the courage to act quickly and imaginatively.

Hollywood on the Liffey happened before in the 1960s. But this time it seems more firmly rooted. It's not dependent on the vagaries of international productions choosing Ireland as a location. It's motored by Ireland's own movie-producing skills and creative drive.

"After years of banging our heads against a brick wall, I think there's a reasonable basis for optimism," says Ardmore boss Kevin Moriarty.

"The difficulty in the past was that no matter how good the scripts coming out of Ireland might be or how talented the people, unless they could bring money to the budget it was very difficult to strike a deal. Now with Section 35 and the Film Board, they can enter into a successful co-production relationship." It's got so that a House of Commons select committee, set up to consider ways of reviving Britain's ailing film industry, visited Dublin to see how that Irish system operated. Says *Commitments* director Alan Parker, who earlier appeared before the Committee with Ken Loach and Mike Leigh: "While the Irish have sorted out the whole thing with ten minutes of legislation, why can't this bunch of idiots do the same?"

Even Jack Valenti, Hollywood's hatchet-man in the GAAT free-trade dispute over attempts to check the dominance of American movies at the European box-office, has turned up in Dublin for talks with Michael D Higgins. At a party given by Jean Kennedy Smith at the Ambassador's residence in Phoenix Park, Valenti congratulates Jordan on the success of *Interview With a Vampire*: "I was at the LA premiere, but I didn't want to intrude on you." "You should have, Jack," Jordan reassures him. "Yeah," says Valenti, "it's a brilliant job. The numbers are right."

Valenti sees the Irish way of making movies as the way forward for Europe. "In terms of investment per film produced, Ireland is now second only to the US," he says. "Instead of taxing its citizens to pour funds into audio-visual, Ireland uses its financial incentives to entice investments to expand the economy. Instead of building walls, Ireland boosts competition. Instead of neglecting the needs of its national audience, Ireland exalts them."

In Dublin also for a major meeting is the European Film Academy — which is even considering moving its base to Ireland. "Ireland is the only country in Europe where something is happening," says its president, the German director Wim Wenders. "This is extremely important, not only for Irish film-makers, but for Europe."

To sustain the momentum, Higgins is considering proposals to set up a film commission to attract movies to Ireland, building on his ad hoc success with *Braveheart*. Another urgent need is the establishment of comprehensive audio-visual training facilities. "We have crewing for perhaps three or four films in Ireland," says Moriarty. "But now we have so many films shooting that it's become necessary to bring in crews. It's no good creating job opportunities if we can't fill them ourselves."

There have been hiccups. The collapse of *Divine Rapture* in mid-production at Ballycotton, despite a dream cast of Marlon Brando, Debra Winger and Johnnny Depp, set off shock waves. But the failure was in the New York financing company CineFin and Los Angeles distributors Orion. No Section 35 money was lost. Nevertheless Higgins is review the operation of Section 35 and admits that it needs retuning.

"The great thing about what Michael D is doing is that it's on an ongoing basis," says Moriarty. "It's not just a quick fix. He wants to continually review what's going on."

Whatever about the disappointments and false dawns of the past, *Ardmore: The Sequel* seems set to run and run.

CHAPTER SEVEN

EPILOGUE

Come with me to a cemetery. Imagine a wall on which the casualties of war are inscribed. Let's read the names...

Bergman's *Shame*, Boorman's *Leo The Last*, Anderson's *If...*, Resnais's *The War Is Over*, Nichols' *The Graduate*, Newman's *Rachel Rachel*, Truffaut's *Stolen Kisses*, Polanski's *Rosemary's Baby*, Schlesinger's *Midnight Cowboy*, Bergman's *A Passion*, Pasolini's *Theorem*, Nichols' *Catch 22*, Makayevich's *Diary of a Switchboard Operator*, Widerberg's *Adalen 31*, Antonioni's *Zabriskie Point*, Yates' *John And Mary*, Bergman's *The Rite*, Altman's *MASH*, Russell's *The Music Lovers*, Lean's *Ryan's Daughter*, Peckinpah's *The Wild Bunch*, Visconti's *The Damned*, Roeg's *Performance*, Cassavetes' *Husbands*, Schlesinger's *Sunday Bloody Sunday*, Russell's *The Devils*, Rafelson's *Five Easy Pieces*, Loach's *Family Life*, Pakula's *Klute*, Bergman's *The Touch*, Fosse's *Cabaret*, Hitchcock's *Frenzy*, Peckinpah's *Straw Dogs*, Fellini's *Satyricon*, Woody Allens *Bananas*...

The roll call from Ireland's censorship war is long and shameful.

But in the end the war was won. Well, sort of. The Government responded to public pressure. More liberal censors were appointed. Few movies now experience any difficulty. But the apparatus of censorship set up in 1923 and consolidated with various legislative amendments, is still in place. It can be reactivated with its full repressive force at the whim of government.

According to the American director Oliver Stone, his 1994 movie *Natural Born Killers* is intended as an indictment of the media's opportunist role in fomenting the modern culture of violence. Critics and commentators have accused him in turn of hypocrisy. They say *Natural Born Killers* is a dangerous movie that in fact glorifies what it attacks.

The debate is important. It raises disturbing issues of social responsibility and creative freedom. It is not, however, a debate to which most people in Ireland have been in a position to make any meaningful contribution. They are in effect prohibited by law from arriving at an informed opinion. *Natural Born Killers* was banned by Film Censor's office. The Appeals Board upheld the banning. This means that Stone's movie is officially regarded as "subversive of public morality". For as long as the ban is in effect — and it cannot be re-appealed for at least seven years — any public screening will be deemed by the courts to be a criminal offence.

Film censorship in Ireland was put on an increasingly reasonable and liberal basis after the appointment of Dermot Breen as Censor in 1972. His successors Frank Hall and now Sheamus Smith, former boss of Ardmore Studios, have cut and banned fewer and fewer movies. Smith in effect functions as a register of movies rather than as a Censor. He rarely cuts and has banned only a handful of movies for the cinema in nearly a decade — the Cynthia Payne biopic *Personal Services*, Ken Russell's *Whore*, Abel Ferrara's *Bad Lieutenant* and now *Natural Born Killers*.

An argument of sorts can be made by him for banning *Natural Born Killers*, which is based on an original screenplay which Quentin Tarantino has since disowned. It has been suggested that several copycat killings have already been inspired by *Natural Born Killers*. There are fears that dysfunctional Mickey, who meets and falls in love with dysfunctional and sexually abused Mallory, slays her parents (drowning dad in a fish bowl, setting mom on fire) and then embarks with her on a wanton

Badlands-style killing spree which turns them into instant media celebrities, will be taken up as a role model by some disturbed youngsters.

Although police involved in most of the cases quoted have discounted an causal connection, some of the evidence is hard to explain away. On 30 October 1994, in Salt Lake city Utah, Nathan Martinez, after seeing *Natural Born Killers* several times, loaded up his .22 and shot dead his stepmother and half-sister. "He thought *Natural Born Killers* was great, it psyched him up," his friend is quoted as saying.

Whatever validity there might be in taking this as a justification for banning *Natural Born Killers*, it cannot be applied to the Irish banning. Because, as is often the case in Ireland, the banning in effect is not a banning at all, but rather an elitist restriction. The 1995 Dublin Film Festival screening of *Natural Born Killers* was a sell-out among movie-goers prepared to pay the £2.50 membership which exempts programmes at the Festival from censorship requirements on the ground that they are not public screenings. *Natural Born Killers* was booked for an "unlimited run" at the Irish Film Centre, again on the basis that audiences would be paying a membership fee in addition to the admission.

The absurd implication is that *Natural Born Killers* is liable to trigger violent responses only in those who do not have access to the Film Festival or the Irish Film Centre (which is rather like the judge in the *Lady Chatterley's Lover* obscenity trial in the 1960s objecting not the hardback but to the cheaper paperback edition of DH Lawrence's great novel on the grounds that it might fall into the hands of servants).

On being confronted with this argument, the Department of Justice reacted with a heavy-handedness reminiscent of their actions in 1972 following the screening of Warhol's *Lonesome Cowboys*. They threatened to have the gardai close down the Irish Film Centre if the screening went ahead. The Irish Film Centre, which is funded by the Arts Council, backed down. The so-called "gentleman's agreement" which has enabled film societies, clubs and festival to operate free of censorship has been put in doubt. Perhaps it will be for the better.

The presumption of any democratic society has to be that all adult citizens — and not just members of clubs — are mature enough to read and view whatever they choose without paternalistic supervision. This is not to say that movies — like books, television, religious sermons or other verbal and visual communications — are not capable of influencing behaviour in a harmful way.

It may well be that *Natural Born Killers* was at least a factor in finally setting off the murderous frustration and hate in Nathan Martinez, a human bomb waiting to go off. But cinema cannot be regulated and restricted on the basis of worst-case scenarios. Disturbed and psychologically unbalanced individuals are liable to be motivated by virtually any stimulus, no matter how tenuous or innocuous. For instance, most murders and crimes of violence occur in domestic situations. Is this a reason for restricting the freedom of people to marry or live together?

Even if *Natural Born Killers* were the kind of gratuitously violent movie it's alleged to be, the argument against banning it would still apply. Stone has delivered an explosive and audacious Swiftian rant against the media for what he claims to be its systematic exploitation of real-life violence in order to boost circulation and ratings. To avoid falling into the same trap himself, he adopts a deliberately unrealistic satirical form: the entire movie is an outrageous pastiche of virtually every know soap-opera stereotype. It's a cerebral rather than a visceral experience, shot in a bewildering melange of colour and black-and-white, handheld Super 8 and widescreen 35mm, the action intercut with cartoon references, clips from newsreels of Hitler and from movies notorious for their depiction of violence (*Midnight Express, The Wild Bunch, Scarface, Frankenstein*).

The effect is to distance the audience from Mickey and Mallory, the murderous couple played by Woody Harrelson and

Juliette Lewis, so that they are seen as prototypes rather than flesh and blood people. They exist only as illustrations of the process by which the media is apt to turn actual killers into vicarious prime-time viewing entertainment.

Natural Born Killers might itself be seen to be cashing in on violence. It has been produced within the mainstream Hollywood system by backers who expect to reap profits from their investment. But this is the only way Stone can operate as a film-maker. It is the only way he can deliver his argument to a mass audience. He is subverting the media from within. It is an honourable creative tradition. Natural Born Killers is an honourable movie.

UK tabloids reacted predictably by attempting to demonise both *Natural Born Killers* and Stone personally. The *Daily Mail* ran front page headlines and editorials on Why This Film Must Be Banned From Britain. Stone was branded as a hypocrite and worse. Even the up-market *The Independent* seems to have been caught up in the hysteria. In a feature page article labelling *Natural Born Killers* as "emblematic of masculine fundamentalism in the 1990s", Beatrice Campbell states that "Stone, too, has a reputation for tyrannical tantrums, frenzy, womanising and bad manners." Whatever Stone might be as a man, his personal life is surely irrelevant to the merits or otherwise of his work.

It has to be said that UK critics generally have treated *Natural Born Killers* dismissively. The pseudo-happy ending which has Mickey and Mallory ludicrously escaping during a prison riot transmitted live on TV and later ending up an archetypal mobile home family with cute children wallowing in junk food and junk culture — the American Dream fulfilled — has been pedantically taken literally as glamorising the violence Stone claims to be condemning.

This is a wilful misreading of the whole thrust of the movie. From start to finish it employs blatantly cliched situations and characterisations to demonstrate the insidious process by which

TV in particular appropriates real-life violence — Waco, Lorena Bobbit, OJ Simpson, Rodney King, the Menendez brothers — and recycles it as soap opera ("they always leave a clerk to tell the tale," gushes the voice-over to a 'reconstructed' film of a drugstore shootout). Mickey and Mallory perceive each other and are perceived throughout purely in these terms. Their abused childhood is observed in flashback as a manic 'I Love Mallory' family sitcom, complete with mindless audience laughter cued to the gross antics of Mallory's perverted dad ("You haven't touched me for fifteen years," her mother complains to him. "What about last night?" "That doesn't count. You were so drunk you thought you were in Mallory's room"). The violence, although luridly explicit, is so fast and fragmented, not to say over-the-top, that it's no more real than a comic strip. The high decibal overlay of such diverse music as Puccini's 'Madama Butterfly', Leonard Cohen's 'Waiting For the Miracle' and Lou Reed's 'Sweet Jane' heightens this alienation effect.

The couple's appalling exploits are instantly mythologised in a massively promoted 'American Maniacs' TV series, hosted by an odious, self-serving Robert Downey Jr., who secures exclusive rights to interview the couple 'live' in prison (his scoop is trailered during the Super Bowl: "Stay tuned...")

"So what next for the Knoxes?" he asks, cosily.

"I'm thinking of motherhood," replies Mallory, drawing an affected "Ah" of approval from the watching crew.

When Michey and Mallory are reunited for the cameras, Downey exclaims unctuously: "This kiss has been a year coming."

Soundbites from instant experts are intercut: "Mickey and Mallory know the difference between right and wrong," opines a psychologist. "They just don't care."

Natural Born Killers is a rare and daring attempt to challenge audiences to look at themselves looking at movies and question what they see. The odium that has been heaped on it is perhaps a measure of its effectiveness. With some justice Stone has said:

"If Robert Downey had been a real-life journalist, then he would have been right in there leading the charge against the movie."

And now twenty years after we thought the battle against film censorship had been more or less won in Ireland, here I am back in the ritual of arguing against the banning of a movie.

I find myself on the platform in a public debate at the Irish Film Centre putting the case that *Natural Born Killers* is not subversive of public morality, but that censorship is.

Of course Ireland hasn't regressed to the dark 1960s, when virtually every movie that mattered was either cut or banned. The Censor, Sheamus Smith, is a civilised and tolerant man. The banning of *Natural Born Killers* can perhaps be dismissed as a momentary aberration.

The worry is that although Smith may rarely feel impelled to apply it, the power to repress cinema is still in force. It is an authoritarian anachronism that hardly belongs in a country that aspires to make an innovative contribution to world cinema.